SCIENC

Made Simple

Preschool/Kindergarten

Help youngsters experience the wonders of science with *The Best Of The Mailbox® Science Made Simple.* This compilation of teaching units and magazine features—selected from 1990 to 1995 issues of *The Mailbox®* magazine for preschool/kindergarten teachers—will enhance your curriculum and introduce basic science skills. Inside this invaluable classroom resource, you'll find:

- Science-based thematic units with across-the-curriculum activities
- Activities that encourage students' active participation
- Helpful ideas for science centers
- Independent and small-group activities
- Background information
- Literature links
- Reproducibles
- Patterns

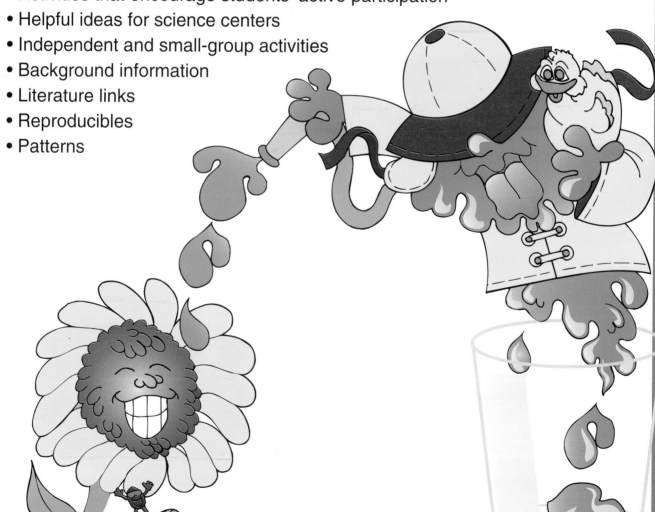

Editors:
Jayne Gammons
Angie Kutzer

Artists:
Pam Crane
Teresa Davidson
Lucia Kemp Henry
Susan Hodnett
Rebecca Saunders
Barry Slate

Cover Artist:
Jennifer Tipton Bennett

Table Of Contents

www.themailbox.com

©1997 by THE EDUCATION CENTER, INC.
All rights reserved.
ISBN# 1-56234-194-4

Manufactured in the United States
10 9 8 7 6 5 4

"Tree-mendous"

A multidisciplinary unit on trees and leaves

by Lucia Kemp Henry

We Need Trees

Leafy trees are very important for the health of our environment. Share some of these interesting facts with your students so they can develop an appreciation for how much we really need our leafy neighbors.

- Trees take in carbon dioxide. In return, they give off the oxygen that people breathe.
- Trees cool the air. They allow water to evaporate from their leaves, which cools the air around them.
- Because the hairy leaf surfaces of trees trap and filter dust and pollen, they reduce air pollution.
- Trees reduce noise pollution by acting as natural sound barriers.
- Tree roots prevent erosion.
- For wildlife, trees are a source of food and shelter.
- Trees provide cool shade for protection from the sun on hot days.
- Trees produce foods, such as fruits and syrup.
- Trees reduce the velocity of strong winds.
- Trees make our world a beautiful place to live by camouflaging unsightly things, by varying their color, and by producing beautiful blooms.

Learning Centers With Leaves

Quickly create some practical centers, using construction-paper leaf cutouts in a variety of shapes, sizes, and colors.

- For a Concentration-type game, cut out several different pairs of leaves. Glue each of the leaves to a separate tagboard card. Have students place the cards facedown and attempt to turn over matching leaf pairs.
- Number a supply of leaf cutouts; then glue them to tagboard cards. To use these leaf cards, have students arrange them in numerical order.
- Glue leaf cutouts to tagboard cards. Cut each card in half. Mix up the card halves. To use the cards, have students find the matching halves.
- Glue several leaf cutouts to each of several sentence strips to establish patterns. To use these pattern strips with a supply of loose leaves, have students manipulate the leaves to repeat or continue each pattern.

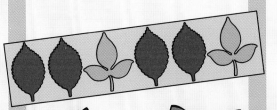

Leaves Everywhere

Cut out a supply of leaf shapes for your students to use when completing their choice of the following projects:

- Decorate construction-paper headbands with the leaf cutouts.
- Cut the center from a paper plate. Glue leaf cutouts around the plate rim to make a decorative wreath.

- Lightly sponge-print each leaf with a contrasting color. To make a classroom tree, glue or tape the painted leaves to a bare tree branch secured in a large container.
- Border a bulletin board with sponge-painted leaf cutouts.
- Create a leaf-shaped nametag to be worn on a field trip to a local nursery or tree farm.

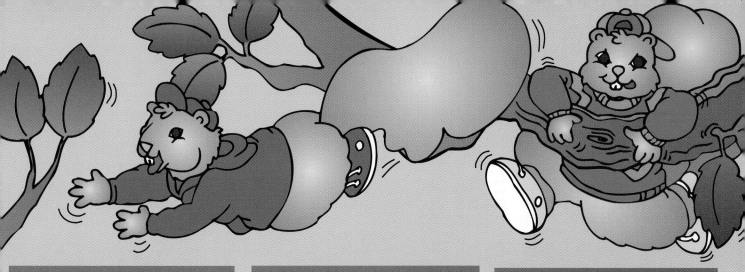

Fall Splendor

Red Leaf, Yellow Leaf by Lois Ehlert (Harcourt Brace Jovanovich, Publishers) is perfect for introducing tree information to young children. Read the book aloud and discuss each of the collages. Share some of the factual information found at the back of the book. If possible, display real leaves, buds, roots, bark, and seeds of a maple tree. Then encourage each student to make leaf artwork for display. To make red and yellow leaves, finger-paint one sheet of finger-paint paper red and another yellow. When the paint is dry, trace an enlarged maple-leaf shape on each sheet. Cut on the resulting outlines. Collect the leaves painted by your students, and tape them on and around a tree cutout to create a huge tree full of bright fall foliage.

Changing The Perspective

Trees can be special in many ways. This lovely book celebrates all the things a tree can be. After reading aloud *Hello, Tree!* by Joanne Ryder (Lodestar Books), take your youngsters outside or visit a local park. Ask students to locate a big, leafy tree. Ask them to lie down on towels in a big circle under the tree, so that their feet are toward the tree's trunk and they can clearly observe the tree's canopy. Encourage each youngster to say a word that describes something about the tree. Jot down the students' descriptions of the tree.

Classifying Leaves

Just as Joanne Ryder's *Hello, Tree!* (Lodestar Books) points out, tree leaves come in many shapes and sizes. Ask your youngsters to collect many different types of tree leaves. Divide students into several small groups, and give each group a variety of leaves. Assist the students in each group as they sort their leaves according to similar characteristics. For example, students may sort their leaves by shape (round, skinny), by color (red, yellow), by texture (smooth, rough), or by size (large, small). Have youngsters glue several samples of each category of leaf to a large sheet of paper. Before putting the papers on display, label (or have students label) each with a category.

"What Grows On Trees?" Booklet

As each youngster compiles his own tree booklet, he'll explore answers to the question, "What grows on trees?" Duplicate the booklet cover and pages (see pages 7–9) on white construction paper for each youngster, and cut apart the pages. If full-size booklet pages are desired, enlarge each booklet page design using a photocopier; then make multiple copies. Begin by asking each child to color his booklet cover and personalize it. On page one of the booklet, have each student glue one or more real or paper leaves in the available space, before coloring the remainder of the page as desired. To complete his copy of booklet page two, ask each student to color as desired, then glue crumpled balls of tissue paper or add sponge-print shapes to represent flowers. On page three, have each child draw fruit (or attach fruit stickers) before coloring the page. To complete page four of the booklet, ask each student to draw people, animals, birds, or insects who benefit from the life of the tree. As each student dictates, write his completion for the incomplete sentence on booklet page five. Assist each youngster in assembling his booklet.

My Tree Book

Tree Hotel

Help your youngsters understand the importance of trees as homes for animals with this fun activity. Begin by reading aloud *Tree Trunk Traffic* by Bianca Lavies (E. P. Dutton). This photograph-illustrated book introduces some familiar animals that depend on trees for protection. Discuss how the tree helps each animal.

Draw a simple picture of a tree, complete with canopy, trunk, and roots. Label the picture with the words "The Tree Hotel." Label the roots, trunk, and canopy with the words "basement," "first floor," and "top floor" respectively. Ask students to name animals that might live on each floor of their tree hotel. For example, worms, lizards, and skunks might live in the basement of the tree, while raccoons and birds inhabit the first floor, and other birds and squirrels have the run of the top floor. Have students draw or cut out pictures of animals and glue them to the appropriate areas of the tree.

Tree Things Collage

Organize a nature hunt to collect tree twigs, leaves, and seeds. Also ask your youngsters to collect these things from their yards at home. Once your collection has reached a suitable size, have your students sort the collection into three different boxes labeled "twigs," "leaves," and "seeds." Starting with a large sheet of construction paper, have each youngster glue on his choice of items from your collections to make a collage. Display all of the collages on a bulletin board titled "Twigs, Leaves, And Seeds."

Tiny Trees

This simple craft project will give each of your little ones an opportunity to create a tiny tree for a tabletop display. To make one, draw a simple canopy shape on white construction paper. Cut out the canopy, and paint or sponge-paint it on both sides. To make the tree's trunk, use a brown or black marker to make a barklike effect on a toilet-paper tube. Cut slits along one end of the tube as shown. Then insert the tree canopy in the trunk by sliding it into the slits. Have each student display his tree on a tabletop with those of his classmates. Encourage youngsters to add small plastic animals to the display and use it to role-play life in the forest.

Did It Begin As A Tree?

Display several objects such as a pencil, a book, a T-shirt, an apple, a metal can, a wooden toy, a plastic toy, a box of tissues, a small plastic milk jug, and a carrot. Hold up the items one at a time, and find out whether students believe a tree was involved in their production. After discussing tree-related products, explain to students that anything made of wood or paper started with a tree. If possible, show students a fallen tree, a stump, or a cross section cut from a log, so that they can see the wood beneath the tree's bark. Afterwards, have students sort groups of objects to indicate whether or not they were made from or came from a tree.

"Tree-mendous" Reading Material

Crinkleroot's Guide To Knowing The Trees
Written & Illustrated by Jim Arnosky
Published by Bradbury Press

Hello, Tree!
Written by Joanne Ryder
Illustrated by Michael Hays
Published by Lodestar Books

The Oak Tree
Written & Illustrated by Laura Jane Coats
Published by Macmillan

Once There Was A Tree
Written by Natalia Romanova
Illustrated by Gennady Spirin
Published by Dial Books For Young
    Readers

Red Leaf, Yellow Leaf
Written & Illustrated by Lois Ehlert
Published by Harcourt Brace Jovanovich

Tree Trunk Traffic
Written & Photographed by Bianca Lavies
Published by E. P. Dutton

The Tremendous Tree Book
Written by May Garelick and Barbara
    Brenner
Illustrated by Fred Brenner
Published by Four Winds Press

Booklet Page 1

A tree has leaves.

Booklet Cover   Use with "'What Grows On Trees?' Booklet" on page 5.

My Tree Book

by _____

A tree has fruit.

A tree has flowers.

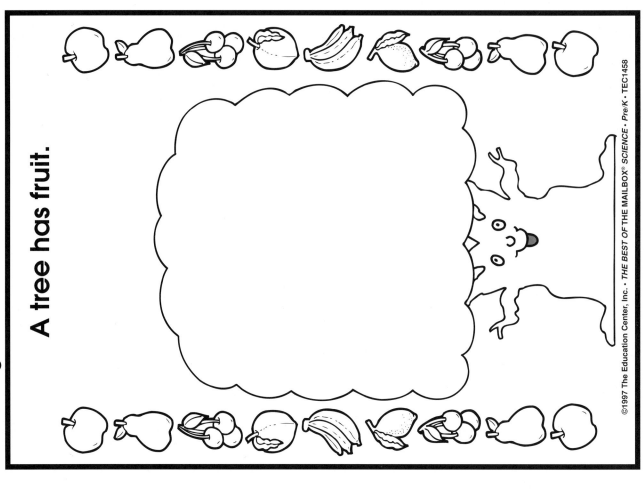

The best thing about trees is...

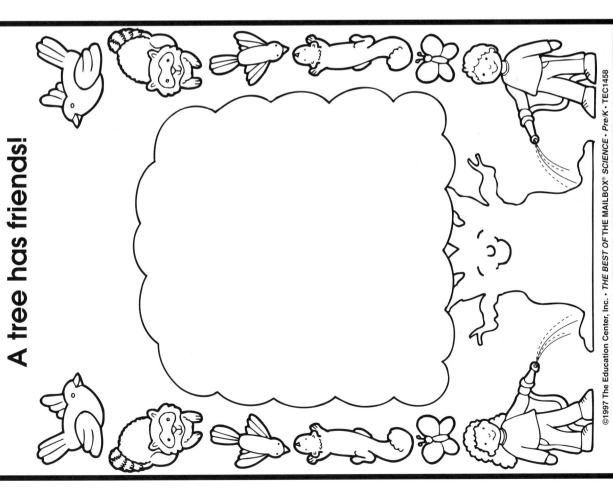

A tree has friends!

Wonders Never Cease

Falling For Leaves

Leaf through this colorful collection of hands-on science activities. Then choose your favorites and invite your youngsters to jump right in. You'll have bushels of fun!

by Lori Bruce

Pam Crane

Activity 1

You will need:
brown lunch sacks (one per child)
freshly fallen leaves
white construction-paper squares
glue
bulletin-board paper

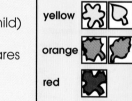

What to do:
Give each youngster a lunch sack. Take youngsters outside and ask them to collect freshly fallen leaves and place them in their sacks. Bring youngsters back inside. Then have them remove their leaves from their sacks and examine them.

Questions to ask:
1. What do you notice about the leaves?
2. Why aren't all of the leaves the same?

Then:
Have each youngster glue his favorite leaf onto a construction-paper square. To create a graph, program a length of bulletin-board paper similarly to the one shown. Then have each youngster glue his square to the appropriate section of the graph.

Questions to ask:
1. How many leaves are red (yellow, orange)?
2. Which color has the most (the least) leaves?

Activity 2

You will need:
a variety of freshly fallen leaves
red, yellow, and orange paint
paintbrushes
poster-board squares (two per child)
pencils

What to do:
Have each youngster personalize the backs of two poster-board squares. Then, to create a leaf print, have each youngster paint the underside of a leaf and press it onto the front of one of his squares. Have the youngster make an identical print on his remaining square. When the prints are dry, store them in a basket. A youngster matches two squares, then turns them over to check. Youngsters can also sort the squares by color, shape, or size, or use them for seriation activities.

Questions to ask:
1. What do you notice about the shapes of the leaves?
2. Why do you think the leaves are different shapes?

This is why:
Leaves are different sizes, shapes, and colors. In the fall, shorter days and cooler nights cause chlorophyll (a green pigment) to break down. The leaves then show their yellow, orange, red, or purple pigments.

This is why:
Each kind of tree has its own special kind of leaves. Deciduous trees (trees that shed their leaves) have leaves that are smooth, toothed (like maple leaves), or lobed (like oak leaves).

Activity 3

You will need:
one-inch coffee filter strips (one per child)
pencils
freshly picked green leaves
Popsicle sticks (one per child)
a jar
rubbing alcohol

What to do:
Have youngsters personalize the tops of coffee filter strips. Then have each youngster position a leaf horizontally across his strip about two inches from the bottom. Using a Popsicle stick, have each youngster gently rub his leaf to transfer some of its pigments onto his strip. Pour rubbing alcohol into the jar so that it is about one inch deep; then have each youngster insert his strip into the jar. Leave the strips in the jar for about 30 minutes; then have youngsters remove them and set them aside to dry. Discard the alcohol.

Questions to ask:
1. What do you see on your strip?
2. Why do you think the streak is yellow?

This is why:

A green spot and a yellow streak formed on the strip. Leaves contain several color pigments. As the alcohol moved up the strip, it dissolved and separated the green and yellow pigments. When we look at a leaf, we see the green pigment, chlorophyll, because there is more of it. Other color pigments are present, too, but they are masked by the chlorophyll. In the fall a leaf stops producing chlorophyll and we can see its other color pigments.

Activity 4

You will need:
an assortment of freshly fallen leaves
waxed paper
crayon shavings (in fall colors)
newspaper
an iron
scissors
a hole puncher
yarn
small twigs (one per child)

What to do:
Have each youngster arrange several leaves on a sheet of waxed paper, then add a sprinkling of crayon shavings. Place a second sheet of waxed paper on top of each youngster's creation; then place the sheets between layers of newspaper. Press the sheets together with an iron set on medium. Remove the sheets from the newspaper and let them cool. Have each youngster cut loosely around each of his leaves and punch a hole in the top of each cutout. Help each youngster tie each of his cutouts to a twig with a length of yarn; then suspend his mobile from the ceiling.

To follow up this activity, discuss composting with your youngsters. Then have youngsters take any leftover leaves back outside and place them in the woods or in a nearby compost pile.

Questions to ask:
1. What are some things people do with leaves in the fall?
2. What do you think happens to leaves that fall in the woods?
3. What is composting?
4. Why do you think people should compost leaves?

This is why:

In the fall people may rake, blow, or burn leaves. Leaves that are left in the woods begin to be broken down into simple substances that provide food for plants. People should compost leaves because it saves landfill space and makes food for plants.

Winter, spring, summer, or fall, this collection of hands-on activities and reproducibles is always in season.

TREES FOR ALL SEASONS

Even youngsters who live in the Sun Belt can experience seasonal changes with these unique trees. Cut four large tree trunks from brown bulletin-board paper. Label each tree with the name of a different season before displaying them. After a discussion of the seasons, have youngsters work together to add these seasonal details:

winter—Cut snowflakes from folded white paper or doilies. Attach the snowflakes to the tree's branches and near its trunk to create a "snowdrift."

spring—Attach white or pink cotton balls to the tree's branches to resemble springtime blossoms.

summer—Cut green construction paper to resemble leaves. Attach the cutouts to the tree's branches.

fall—Using yellow, orange, red, and brown paint, sponge-print a length of white bulletin-board paper. When the paint is dry, cut or tear the paper to resemble leaves. Attach the "leaves" to the tree's branches and in a cluster near its trunk.

Cathy McDougal, Palm Coast, FL

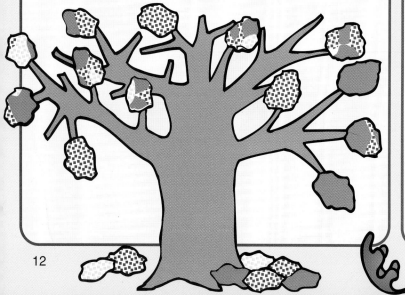

THE FOUR SEASONS

Youngsters won't soon forget this action-packed introduction to the four seasons. In unison, have youngsters name the four seasons while performing the following movements:

fall—Drop to the ground.

winter—Stand up and shiver while clutching shoulders.

spring—Jump up.

summer—Fan face with hands while pretending to be very hot.

Beth Riley—Pre-K, Precious Moments Nursery School Gloucester, NJ

HIBERNATION HOOPLA

During your study of fall, help youngsters grasp the concept of hibernation with this hands-on activity. Have each youngster bring a stuffed animal (one that he can bear to part with for a few months) to school. Have a few extra stuffed animals on hand for those youngsters who are unable to bring one from home. After a discussion about hibernation, place the animals in a box labeled "Shhh! Animals Sleeping." Set the box on a high shelf or in a closet until February. Imagine your youngsters' delight when they enter the classroom on Groundhog Day to find their animals "awake" and ready to greet them.

Deborah Harbin—Transition, Emmott Elementary Houston, TX

SURPRISES

SEASON TICKET

This simple rhyme is just the ticket for helping youngsters associate each season with its weather:
Summer is hot.
Spring is nice.
Fall is cool.
Winter is ice.

Where, oh where do the bears sleep when the snow is deep?

Winter Houses
Deon

WINTER WONDERS

During winter, some animals hibernate, while others adapt to the cold weather in other ways. To help youngsters understand what happens to living creatures during winter, duplicate student copies of house-shaped booklet pages, each programmed with one of the following verses:

*Where, oh where do the beavers go
when it begins to snow?
Where, oh where do the bears sleep
when the snow is deep?
Where, oh where do the rabbits hide
when it's cold outside?
Where, oh where do the deer stay
when it's too cold to play?
Where, oh where do I go when the wind starts to blow?
My house! It's the very best house of all!*

After a discussion about hibernation and other ways living creatures adapt to winter, have each child cut out and illustrate his copy of each booklet page. Staple each child's pages between house-shaped, construction-paper covers; then have him decorate his front cover as shown.
*Monica Campbell—Pre-K
The Lexington School
Lexington, KY*

PAPER BAG PLANTIN'

When spring plantin' time comes, much of nature's work takes place underground. For a revealing look at the underground life of plants, have each youngster decorate the upper portion of a paper bag with an illustration of a carrot plant as shown. Then have him fold down the flap and illustrate the carrot root in the ground. As a variation, have youngsters draw flowers above the "ground" and roots or bulbs "underground." Little gardeners will enjoy manipulating the flap to discover the underground surprise
*Janet Skipper—Gr. K, Roseland Park
School, Picayune, MS*

ON THE WINGS OF SUMMER

Youngsters emerge as beautiful, summer butterflies from this hands-on experience. To simulate the life cycle of a butterfly, have a youngster lie on the floor with his hands at his sides and wiggle, imitating a caterpillar. Then have the "caterpillar" loosely wrap himself in a sheet (chrysalis). After a few seconds, have the "butterfly" emerge from its chrysalis, spread its "wings," and "take flight."
*Brenda A. Lehman, Children's Garden
Morristown, NJ*

13

CIRCLE OF SEASONS

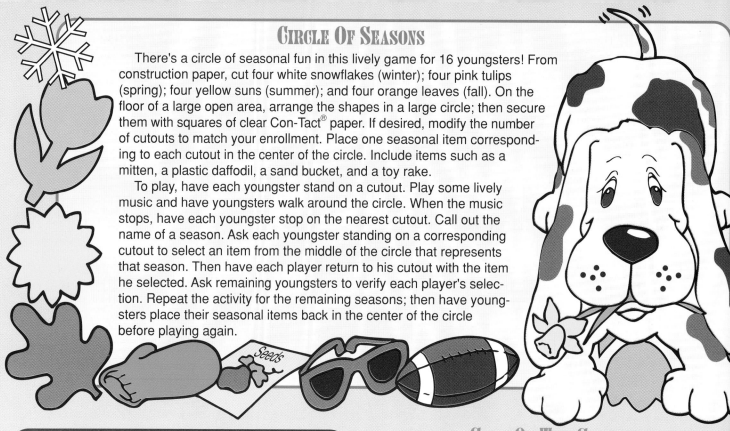

There's a circle of seasonal fun in this lively game for 16 youngsters! From construction paper, cut four white snowflakes (winter); four pink tulips (spring); four yellow suns (summer); and four orange leaves (fall). On the floor of a large open area, arrange the shapes in a large circle; then secure them with squares of clear Con-Tact® paper. If desired, modify the number of cutouts to match your enrollment. Place one seasonal item corresponding to each cutout in the center of the circle. Include items such as a mitten, a plastic daffodil, a sand bucket, and a toy rake.

To play, have each youngster stand on a cutout. Play some lively music and have youngsters walk around the circle. When the music stops, have each youngster stop on the nearest cutout. Call out the name of a season. Ask each youngster standing on a corresponding cutout to select an item from the middle of the circle that represents that season. Then have each player return to his cutout with the item he selected. Ask remaining youngsters to verify each player's selection. Repeat the activity for the remaining seasons; then have youngsters place their seasonal items back in the center of the circle before playing again.

SEASONAL FLIP BOOKLETS

Youngsters will flip for these seasonal booklets. For booklet covers, cut two 5 1/2-inch construction-paper squares for each child. Then duplicate student copies of page 15. Have each youngster cut out and color the booklet pages and cover emblem. To complete the booklet, have each youngster glue his cover emblem atop a 5 1/2-inch construction-paper square, then add his name. Assist each youngster in collating his booklet pages as shown. Then staple the pages between each youngster's decorated cover square and an undecorated one.

If your youngsters are big flip booklet fans, follow the directions above to create more flip booklets using copies of page 16. If desired, combine these two smaller booklets into one. How quickly the seasons change!

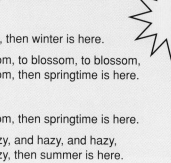

SONG OF THE SEASONS

Culminate your study of the seasons with the singing of this upbeat tune that knows *every* season!

Song Of The Seasons
sung to the tune of "Did You Ever See A Lassie?"

When the icy winds are blowing, are blowing, are blowing,
When the icy winds are blowing, then winter is here.
Snow tickles your nose,
And it freezes your toes.
When the icy winds are blowing, then winter is here.

When the flowers start to blossom, to blossom, to blossom,
When the flowers start to blossom, then springtime is here.
The grass turns so green.
All the birds start to sing.
When the flowers start to blossom, then springtime is here.

When the weather's hot and hazy, and hazy, and hazy,
When the weather's hot and hazy, then summer is here.
Fireworks light up the sky
On the Fourth of July.
When the weather's hot and hazy, then summer is here.

When the colored leaves are falling, are falling, are falling,
When the colored leaves are falling, then autumn is here.
Floating down to the ground.
Red, orange, yellow, and brown.
When the colored leaves are falling, then autumn is here.

MORE SEASONAL SENSATIONS

Season your whole language program with these sensational titles:

- *All Year Long* by Nancy Tafuri
- *A Circle Of Seasons* by Myra Cohn Livingston
- *January Brings The Snow* by Sara Coleridge
- *Mouse Days* by Leo Lionni
- *My Favorite Time Of Year* by Susan Pearson
- *Ox-Cart Man* by Donald Hall, winner of the Caldecott Medal
- *Seasons* by Heidi Goennel
- *Summer Is...* by Charlotte Zolotow
- *Winter* by Ron Hirschi
- *Caps, Hats, Socks, And Mittens* by Louise Borden

summer

winter

Cover Emblem

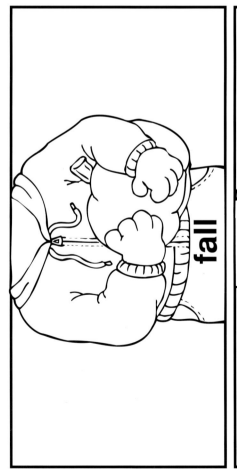

fall

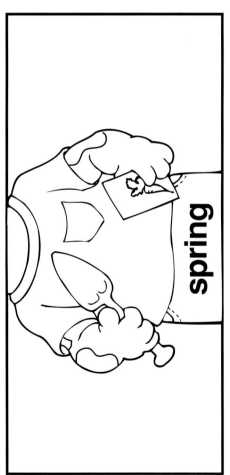

spring

What Will Sooner Wear?

Booklet Pages Use with "Seasonal Flip Booklets" on page 14.

summer

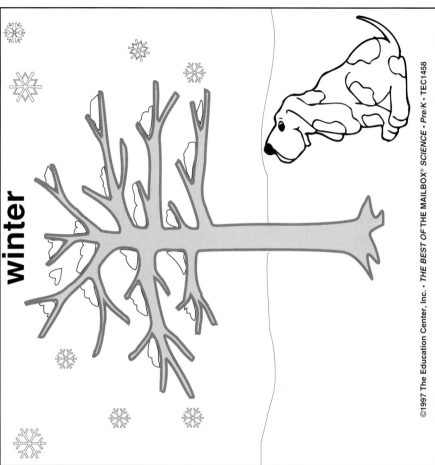

winter

Cover Emblem

Sooner's Seasons

spring

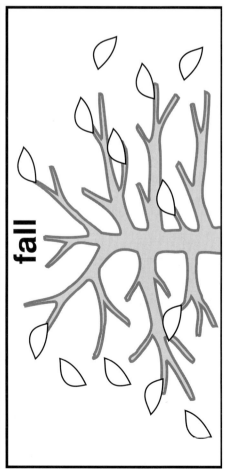

fall

Shadow Escapades

When the bright harvest moon casts mysterious fall silhouettes, it's the perfect time to introduce your youngsters to the secrets of shadows.

Pam Crane

Activity 1

You will need:
a sunny morning

What to do:
In the middle of the morning, take youngsters outside to a sunny, open space. Have each child stand with his back to the sun, then observe his shadow. Have youngsters jump, twist, and wiggle while observing their shadows.

Questions to ask:
- What do you call the dark spot you see on the ground?
- What causes a shadow to appear?
- What happens to your shadow when you move?

This is why:

Shadows are dark spots made by things that do not let a direct light pass through them. When you move, your shadow moves in the same way.

Activity 2

You will need:
a sunny day
a large, open field with a shaded area

What to do:
After youngsters have completed Activity 1, invite them to play shadow tag. To play shadow tag, divide youngsters into two teams. Have one team, Shadows, stand in the "safe zone" (shaded area). Have the members of the other team, Chasers, stand in the middle of the field. When you call, "Run, Shadows, run!" Chasers chase Shadows, attempting to "tag" (step on) their shadows. Youngsters standing in the shaded area cast no shadows, so they are safe. A child is out when his shadow is tagged. Play continues until all Shadows have been tagged. Have teams reverse their roles and play a second round.

Questions to ask:
- How can you make your shadow disappear?
- Why were you safe in the shaded area?

This is why:

A shadow disappears in a shaded area because there is no direct light source.

More Shadowy Surprises

These terrific literature tie-ins are lurking in your local library:

- *Bear Shadow* by Frank Asch
- *I Have A Friend* by Keiko Narahashi

Youngsters with longer attention spans will also enjoy these shadowy tales shared during several sittings:

- *Nothing Sticks Like A Shadow* by Ann Tompert
- *Shadow* by Marcia Brown, winner of the Caldecott Medal
- *The Boy With Two Shadows* by Margaret Mahy, particularly timely at Halloween

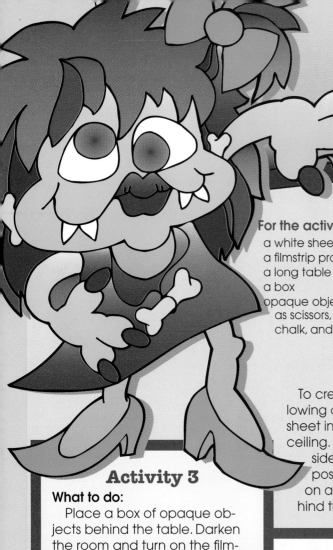

For the activities on this page, you will need:

a white sheet
a filmstrip projector
a long table
a box
opaque objects such
   as scissors, crayons,
   chalk, and pencils

straws (4 per child)
construction-paper
   copies of page 19
   (1 per child)
scissors
tape

To create a stage for the following activities, hang a white sheet in a doorway or from the ceiling. Place a long table on its side behind the sheet; then position a filmstrip projector on a desk or tabletop behind the table.

Activity 3

What to do:

Place a box of opaque objects behind the table. Darken the room and turn on the filmstrip projector. Have youngsters take turns selecting an object from the box and holding it in the light to produce a shadow. Have remaining youngsters identify each object.

Questions to ask:
• Which shadows were the easiest to identify?
• Which shadows were more difficult to identify?

This is why:

Shadows of unique shapes such as scissors are easy to identify. Since shadows are only silhouettes, items having circular, square, or other common shapes are harder to identify.

Activity 4

What to do:

Have a youngster repeat the procedure for Activity 3 as you move the filmstrip projector closer to the object he displays. Then gradually move the projector farther and farther away from the object. Ask youngsters to observe how the shadow changes as you have additional youngsters repeat the procedure using different objects.

Questions to ask:
• What happened to the shadow?
• Why do you think this happened?

This is why:

An object's shadow appears larger when the object is closer to the light source, because it blocks more light. When the light source is farther away, the shadow appears smaller because it blocks less light.

Activity 5

What to do:

Assist each child in cutting out the patterns on his copy of page 19. To create shadow puppets, tape a straw to the back of each cutout. Play some eerie background music while youngsters work in pairs or small groups to create their own shadow puppet shows. Or have youngsters use their puppets to perform shadowy, Halloween finger plays.

Questions to ask:
• Where have you seen shadows?
• What is another way to make shadow puppets?

This is why:

Shadows occur wherever a light source such as the sun or a light bulb shines upon an opaque object. Shadow puppets can also be made using your hands and fingers.

Youngsters will enjoy experimenting to create their own shadow puppets like the one shown below or the ones featured in *Shadow Magic* by Seymour Simon.

Wonders Never Cease

Spinning Ghosts

For these activities you will need:

two sheets of newspaper
a large paper ghost pattern
(page 22) for each student
a medium- and small-sized ghost
pattern for each student (page 23)

scissors
paper clips
crayons

ideas by Margie Dunlevy

Activity 1

Ball up the first of two sheets of newspaper. Leave the other one flat. Drop the two newspaper sheets from a considerable height. For example, if there's a staircase in your building, you can drop the sheets over the handrail to the floor below.

Questions to ask:
- Which sheet hit the ground first?
- Do you think the sheets weigh about the same?
- Why did the balled-up sheet fall faster than the flat paper?

This is why:
Although both pieces of paper have the same weight, the shape of the paper affects the fall. There is more air resistance pushing up against the large surface area of the flat sheet of newspaper than is pressing against the smaller surface of the balled-up sheet of newspaper. So the flat paper's fall is slower.

Activity 2

Have each student cut out the large ghost pattern from page 22 and attach a paper clip to the bottom. Then have each student throw his ghost cutout straight up into the air.

Questions to ask:
- Why didn't the ghost keep on going higher and higher into the air?
- How did the ghost fall?
- What could we do to the ghost to get it to fall slower?

This is why:
Objects that are on or near the earth are pulled toward the earth. When the ghost fell, gravity was pulling it back to earth.

Activity 3

Now have each youngster fold his ghost's arm A forward and arm B backward. Have each student throw his ghost straight up into the air.

Questions to ask:
- Did the ghost fall the same way as it did before?
- What was different about the way it fell?
- Why did bending the arms cause the ghost to fall in a different way?

This is why:
When things fall, the air resists the falling bodies, so they are not falling under the influence of gravity alone. The ghost's fall is slowed because the folded arms create more air resistance than the unfolded arms did.

Activity 4

Have each student throw his ghost straight up. Watching carefully, have students observe which way they spin.

Questions to ask:
- Which way did your ghost spin?
- Did your ghost spin in the same direction that clock hands move?

Activity 5

Have each student change the ghost arms so that arm B is bent forward and arm A is backward. After throwing their ghosts straight up, have students observe which way they spin.

Questions to ask:
- Which way did your ghost spin this time?
- Did it spin in the same direction that clock hands move?
- How is this different from the way the ghost spun before?
- Why would changing the arm folds change the way the ghost spins?

Activity 6

Have each student cut out the medium- and small-sized ghosts from page 23. Put a paper clip on the bottom of each ghost. Fold their arms. Now have students throw each of their ghosts straight up, one at a time.

Questions to ask:
- How do the ghosts' falls differ?
- Why do some ghosts spin more and fall faster than others?

This is why:

The arms of the paper ghost are much like helicopter blades. As the ghost falls, its arms begin to generate lift, causing it to rotate. The weight of the paper clip is balanced by the upward force of lift. The ghost rotates because the weight and lift aren't parallel.

This is why:

Each arm generates lift. But, in flight, the arms are not parallel. The spin is influenced by the deflection of air currents beneath the arms. Reversing the arms reverses the way the air is deflected, causing a spin in the opposite direction.

This is why:

The larger surface of the large ghost's arms and body creates more air resistance than those of the other ghosts. So the larger one spins and falls more slowly. The smaller the arm and body surface, the faster the fall and the spin.

For more fun:
- Have each youngster color his ghosts.
- Have youngsters experiment by adding more paper clips to their ghosts. How does this change the way the ghosts fall?
- Bring in helicopter models, books, and pictures. Have students compare their ghosts' descents to the descents of helicopters.
- Have youngsters collect and experiment with the winged seeds of maple trees. When a paper clip is clipped in the center of the seeds, how does the descent change?
- Put a haunted house cutout at the bottom of a staircase. Have youngsters drop their ghosts off the sides of the stairs in an attempt to land them on the haunted house.

21

Pattern
Use with activities on pages 20 and 21.

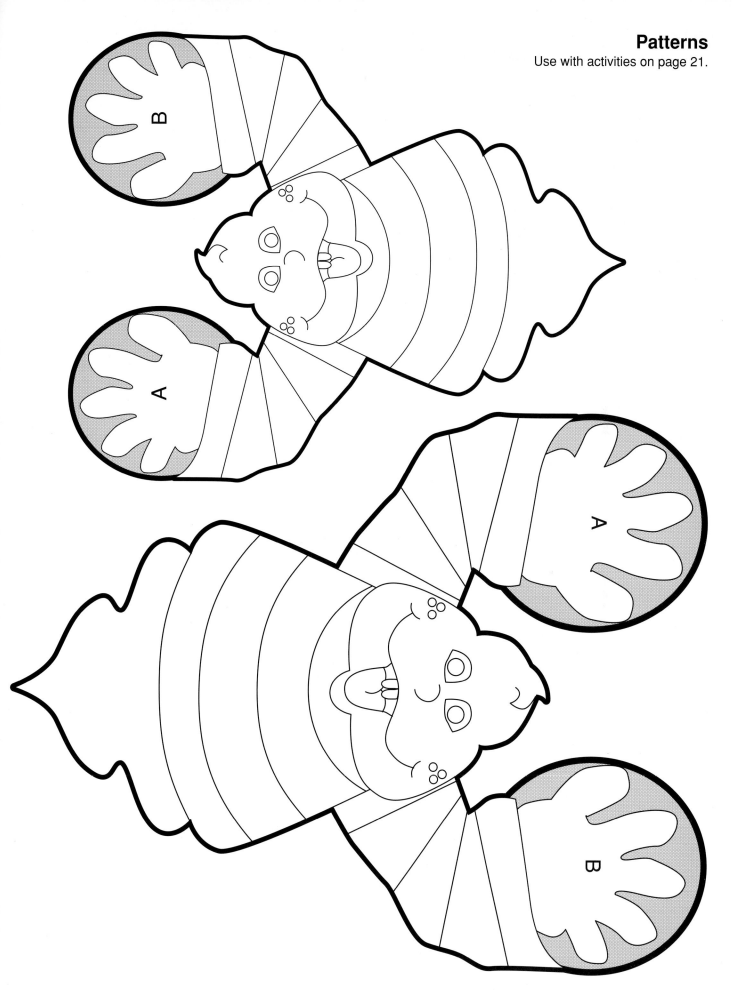

Wonders Never Cease

Something's In The Air!

Your youngsters will breeze through these hands-on activities as they learn about air.

by Marie Iannetti

Activity 1

You will need:
small paper bags (1 per child)
6" pieces of string (1 piece per child)

What to do:
Supply each child with a paper bag and a piece of string. Have each of your youngsters open and examine his bag and its contents carefully.

Questions to ask:
- Is there anything inside the paper bag?
- Could something that you can't see be there?
- Do you think you can see air?
- Do you think you can feel air? How?

What to do:
Have each child gather the bag near the top and hold it so that there's only a small opening. Instruct him to blow into his bag to fill it with air. Have him quickly close the open end of the bag; then assist him as he ties it tightly with his piece of string.

Questions to ask:
- Is there anything in your bag?
- What do you think is in your bag?
- How can you tell there is something there?
- Does your bag feel or look different? How?

Then:
Have each child place his hand on his chest and take a deep breath. Then ask him to let out the air.

Questions to ask:
- What do you think was happening to your lungs when you were breathing in? Why?
- How are filling the bag and filling your lungs the same?

This is how:
Even though you cannot see air, you can see what it does. Air takes up space. You can see or feel air when you put it inside something like a paper bag or your lungs because it takes on the shape of the object that contains it.

For free exploration:
Have your youngsters brainstorm and bring in other objects from home that could be filled with air (such as a self-locking plastic bag, a bottle of bubble solution, a balloon, or an inflatable toy).

Activity 2

You will need:
one of each of the following per small group:
    plastic glass
    paper towel
    large bowl
water

What to do:
Fill the bowls 3/4 full of water. Supply a bowl, paper towel, and plastic glass for each group. Have one child in each group crumple the paper towel and push it deep inside the glass.

Questions to ask: (Graph your students' predictions on chart paper or a chalkboard.)
- Do you think the water will go inside the glass if we place the glass in the bowl?
- What do you think will happen to the paper towel? Why?

What to do:
Have another child in the group turn the glass upside down with the mouth facing downward. Keeping the glass straight, have him push the glass down into the bowl of water. Then have him lift the glass straight up from the bowl. Ask your students to carefully examine the paper towel.

Questions to ask:
- What happened to the paper towel?
- Why do you think the paper towel did not get wet?

This is why:
Because air occupies space, it will push other things out of the way. The air in the glass was trapped inside. The air prevented the water from entering the glass and reaching the paper towel.

Pam Crane

Activity 3

You will need:

one of each of the following per small group:
  large plastic tub or bowl
  water
  glue

one of each of the following per student:
  half-pint milk carton cut in
    half vertically
  Popsicle® stick
  3" construction-paper square
  small ball of clay

What to do:

Seat each small group of youngsters around a table. Supply each child with a Popsicle® stick, milk-carton half, ball of clay, and construction-paper square. To make a boat, have each child press the ball of clay into the milk carton half. Then have him glue the construction-paper square to the Popsicle® stick and push the stick into the ball of clay.

Questions to ask: (Record your students' predictions on chart paper or a chalkboard.)
• If you put your boat in water, how can you move the boat without using your hands?
• Do you think air or wind can move things? Why?

What to do:

Place a tub or bowl on a table for each group. Partially fill each tub with water. In turn, have two students from each group place their boats in the tub. Have them blow against their sails softly. Then have them blow harder against their sails. Have the other students in the group follow the same procedure.

Questions to ask:
• Did your boat move?
• What happened when you blew softly?
• What happened when you blew hard?
• Why did your boat move?

This is why:

Wind is moving air. Moving air can do work such as moving the sailboat from one end of the tub to the other. When you blew air, the air pushing on the sail moved forward. This caused the boat to move.

Just for fun:

On a windy day, take a variety of objects such as a ball, a leaf, an inflated balloon, and a piece of paper outside. Have your youngsters observe how the wind moves these objects and compare their observations.

Activity 4

You will need:

each of the following per small group:
  a yardstick
  3 six-inch pieces of string
  2 inflated balloons (the same size)
  a straight pin
  tape

Questions to ask:
• Do you think air has weight? Why or why not?

What to do:

For each group, place a yardstick, 2 inflated balloons, and 3 strings on a table. Seat a small group of youngsters around each table. Have one child in each group tie a piece of string to the middle of the yardstick. Ask two other children from each group to tie a string to each balloon. Then have another child tape each of the balloons to an end of the yardstick. (Since the position of the balloons and the lengths and positions of the strings can affect the balance, tape the middle string at the middle of the yardstick, and make sure each balloon hangs from the yardstick at the same height and at an equal distance from the nearest yardstick end.) Instruct one student from each group to hold the yardstick by the middle string, so that the yardstick hangs parallel with the floor.

Questions to ask:
• Do you think the air-filled balloons have weight? Why or why not?
• Do you think they both have the same weight? Why or why not?
• What do you think would happen to the yardstick if one of the balloons popped?

Then:

Use a straight pin to deflate one balloon of each pair while the yardstick is suspended by the middle string as before.

Questions to ask:
• What happened to the yardstick?
• Why do you think that happened?
• What does this tell you about air?

This is what happened:

Because both balloons were the same weight, they balanced the yardstick. When one balloon was popped, the weight shifted. Since the yardstick had more weight on the end with the inflated balloon, you could see that the air in the balloon did weigh something.

Awesome Owls

Who-o-o-o can resist the round, fluffy face, huge bright eyes, and wise expression of an owl? Enchant your youngsters with integrated owl activities that they won't be able to resist. This unit includes a song, a fingerplay, art activities, an informational booklet, and literature-based activities.

by Lucia Kemp Henry

I Hadn't Heard

Delight your students by sharing pictures of owls with them and by telling them a few of these facts about owls.

- Owls have the world's best night vision and they can hear better than other birds.
- Owl eyes don't move. But owls have very flexible necks that allow their heads to turn most of the way around (about 270°).
- Ear tufts, although often mistaken for ears, have nothing to do with the owl's hearing. Owls don't have ears that you can usually see. Large ear holes are hidden by their facial disks.
- Owls can pick up sounds better by making small adjustments in the position of their facial disks.
- Unlike most birds, the feathers of an owl's wings have soft edges. This helps an owl fly almost silently, so as not to be heard by its prey.
- Unlike other birds of prey, owls fly very close to the ground.
- Owls are helpful to humans by helping to keep the rodent and insect populations under control.
- Owls can be unfriendly to animals and other birds. To scare an intruder away, an owl will spread its wings, fluff its feathers, and hiss.
- Most owls live in trees, but some have unusual homes like burrows in the ground and cacti.
- Great Gray Owls are bold birds. A Great Gray Owl will sit for hours watching people in the forest.
- Burrowing Owls prefer to move into abandoned prairie dog holes rather than to dig their own. When intruders approach, Burrowing Owls make a sound similar to the warning of a rattlesnake.

"Little Hoot Owl" Song

Most owls are nocturnal. Their huge forward-facing eyes help them see very well in the dark. They use their excellent sight and hearing to hunt rodents and other small animals that are active at night. Teach your youngsters this song, and they'll learn these facts in a fun way.

Little Hoot Owl
(sung to the tune of "Six Little Ducks")

Who flies around in the dark of night?
Who glides on wings of silent flight?
Who eats his dinner by late moonlight?
It's a little hoot owl with his owl eyesight!

Who-who, who-who, little hoot owl.
Who-who, who-who, little hoot owl.
Who-who, who-who, little hoot owl.
It's a little hoot owl with his owl eyesight!

Owl Facts Booklet

There are many different kinds of owls. Some are quite large and others are very, very small. They live in a wide variety of habitats and can be found on every continent except Antarctica. Provide your students with copies of the owl booklet patterns on pages 30–35 to help acquaint them with several North American owls.

Reproduce the booklet patterns on white construction paper for each youngster. Read aloud and discuss the information on each booklet page. Reinforce your discussions with drawings or photos from owl resource books. (One excellent resource choice is Zoobooks *Owls*, which is published by Wildlife Education, Ltd.) Help your youngsters complete each booklet page according to the directions. Then assist them, if necessary, in cutting out each of the booklet pages along the bold outline. To finish each booklet, stack the pages in order and staple them near the left edge. For optional fun, provide small natural-colored feathers (available from a craft store) for students to glue to the owl booklet covers.

Owls

by Keri Jones

Flannelboard Fun

This little rhyme will make counting and owl identification a snap! Cut out the owl flannelboard figures on pages 145 and 147. Back each figure with felt. Then use the owl flannelboard figures to accompany "Five Little Owls."

Five Little Owls

Five little owls on a dark, dark night.
    Five little owls are quite a sight.
Five little owls. Are you keeping score?
    One flies away and that leaves four.
Four little owls as happy as can be.
    One flies away and that leaves three.
Three little owls calling, "Who, who, who!"
    One flies away and that leaves two.
Two little owls having lots of fun.
    One flies away and that leaves one.
One little owl and we're almost done!
    He flies away and that leaves none!

"Who Are You?" Fingerplay

Here's another counting rhyme that will have your youngsters hooting their hearts out!

Way up high in the old oak tree,   *Point up.*
One little hoot owl looked at me.   *Hold up one finger.*
So I said, "Who-who? Oh, who are you?" *Make circles with fingers. Peer through them.*
"Who-who," he said, and away he flew.   *Flap arms.*

Repeat the verse, increasing the number of owls with each repetition and modifying the wording and motions accordingly.

Owl Masks

Have students make these masks from simple materials, then wear them to act out owl songs and poems. To make a mask, begin by duplicating the mask patterns (on page 36) on white construction paper. Color the mask patterns and the back of a thin paper plate. Then cut out each of the patterns. Staple a tagboard strip to opposite sides of the plate for a headband, fitting it for the wearer. Center and glue the eyes/beak cutout on the plate. Then cut out the eyeholes so that the wearer can see through the mask. Carefully cut around the two sides of the beak; then bend the beak upward slightly. Glue the ear tuft cutouts to the upper portion of the mask. "Who-oo-ose" turn is it to be the owl?

Paper-Bag Owls

These stuffed paper owls are perfect for perching on your classroom window ledge. To make a stuffed owl, begin with a brown paper lunch bag. Stuff the bag with newspaper and staple it closed. Cut out construction-paper copies of the owl head and wing designs (on page 36). On the head cutout, draw and color an owl's facial features. Color the head and wings, if desired, with crayons. Glue these pieces to the stuffed paper bag. To simulate fluffy feathers, glue small balls of rolled-up brown, black, and white tissue paper to the front of the owl's breast.

Crayon Resist Owls

These student-made hoot owls will fill an autumn bulletin board with a flock of surprises. To make this project, begin with a construction-paper copy of the owl pattern on page 37. Color in the owl as desired using brown, red, orange, yellow, and white crayons to make feathers, eyes, and a beak. Apply the crayon with dark heavy strokes. Using a wide brush, brush a single coat of very thin black tempera paint or black watercolor over the colored owl. Allow the project to dry before cutting out the design.

Display these student-made owls on a bulletin board with a black, purple, or royal blue background highlighted by a bright yellow paper moon and white paper stars. If desired, have each student dictate something interesting he has learned about owls as you write his dictation on a conversation balloon. Then assist each youngster as he staples his conversation balloon by his owl.

Owl eyes don't move.

Where's My Tree?

Many owls have adapted to contemporary life. But other owls are having trouble keeping or finding a home. As trees are cut down for lumber and land development, some owls (such as the Spotted Owl) have to find other homes to survive. Play a game with your students to point out that animals are sometimes displaced by humans and to get them thinking about what can be done to help the animals.

Divide your students into two equal-size groups, specifying that one group of them are owls and one group of them are trees. Have each tree find a space on the playground and "freeze." Then instruct the owls to randomly "fly" around the trees. Blow a whistle, signaling that each owl must find a tree. Repeat this several times before removing one of the trees from the game. Blow the whistle again. The owl without a tree must sit out the remainder of the game. Continue to remove the trees until only one owl and one tree remain.

Following the game, talk to youngsters about the plight of owls whose trees are cut down. Ask youngsters to think of ways to help the homeless owls. Be sure to mention that laws can help protect owls, wilderness areas can be set aside, and people living near cities can make nestboxes for owls.

Baby Owl Literature

Owl babies are called *chicks.* The chicks usually hatch from their eggs about two days apart. Owl parents are very protective and spend lots of time hunting for food to provide for their young. They teach their chicks to fly and to hunt for food so that the chicks can go off on their own when they are about three months old.

Owl Babies, written by Martin Waddell and illustrated by Patrick Benson (published by Candlewick Press), is a strikingly illustrated story of three owl chicks and their experiences on a dark night. They wake to find that their mother is gone! They are worried about her and wonder what she is doing. Have your youngsters discuss places that the mother owl may have visited. Ask them to decide if she did bring back food, as Sarah Owl suggested. Have students dictate an extended ending to the story, having the mother owl tell where she has been and what she has brought back to the nest.

Owliver, written by Robert Kraus and illustrated by Jose Aruego and Ariane Dewey (published by Windmill Books, Inc.), is a more fanciful tale about an owl chick with a very vivid imagination and a talent for acting. Owliver especially likes to imitate other creatures. Have your youngsters name the birds and animals that Owliver imitates in the story. Ask them to describe the jobs that he acts out as well. Have each child write or dictate a sentence describing one aspect of Owliver's playacting; then combine all of the sentences to create a class story about Owliver.

Owl Books

Owl Babies
Written by Martin Waddell
Illustrated by Patrick Benson
Published by Candlewick Press

Owliver
Written by Robert Kraus
Illustrated by Jose Aruego & Ariane Dewey
Published by Windmill Books, Inc.

Owl
From the "See How They Grow" series
Written by Mary Ling
Published by Dorling Kindersley, Inc.

The Owl Who Became The Moon
Written by Jonathan London
Illustrated by Ted Rand
Published by Dutton Children's Books

Good-Night, Owl
Written & Illustrated by Pat Hutchins
Published by Macmillan Children's Book Group

Owl And The Pussycat
Written by Edward Lear
Illustrated by Jan Brett
Published by G. P. Putnam's Sons

Owl Moon
Written by Jane Yolen
Illustrated by John Schoenherr
Published by Philomel Books

Whoo-oo Is It
Written by Megan McDonald
Illustrated by S. D. Schindler
Published by Orchard Books

Fly By Night
Written by June Crebbin
Illustrated by Stephen Lambert
Published by Candlewick Press

Owl Booklet Cover

by

Color.
Cut out the word.
Glue it to the box.
Write your name.

 ©1997 The Education Center, Inc. • *THE BEST OF* THE MAILBOX® *SCIENCE* • *Pre/K* • TEC1458

Glue moon here.

This is a Great Horned Owl.
It hunts at night.
It has big eyes to help it see in the dark.

1.

Color.
Cut out the moon
    and stars.
Glue them to the
    page.

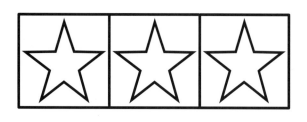

This is a Snowy Owl.
It lives in cold northern lands.
Its thick feathers keep it warm.

2.

Color.
Cut out the snowflakes.
Glue them to the page.

This is a Barn Owl.
It lives near farms and fields.
It eats mice that eat the farmers' crops.

3.

Color.
Cut out the mice.
Glue them to the page.

Glue the
owl here.

These are Burrowing Owls.
They do not live in trees.
They make their homes in underground burrows.

4.

Color.
Cut out the owl.
Glue it to the burrow.

These are Pygmy Owls.
They are very small.
They eat some insects like grasshoppers.

5.

Color.
Cut out the grasshoppers.
Glue them to the page.

Patterns   Use with "Paper-Bag Owls" on page 28.

wings   head

Patterns   Use with "Owl Masks" on page 28.

Glue
behind plate
here.

Glue
behind plate
here.

eyes/beak   ear tufts

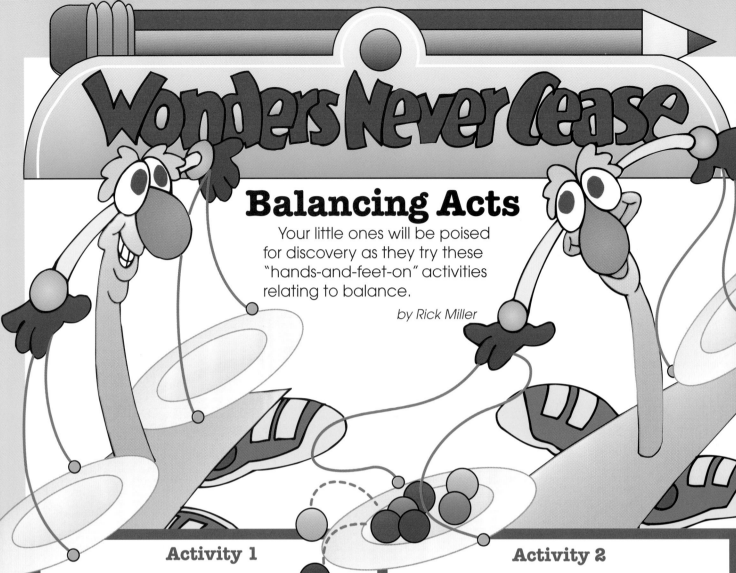

Wonders Never Cease

Balancing Acts

Your little ones will be poised for discovery as they try these "hands-and-feet-on" activities relating to balance.

by Rick Miller

Activity 1

You will need:
a low balance beam
(or a curb; or a long, narrow line on a flat surface)

What to do:
Have each child try to walk along the balance beam. (If a balance beam is not available, have youngsters walk along a curb, or a line such as a crack in a sidewalk, or a chalk line.)

Questions to ask:
• What happens when you try to walk along the balance beam (curb/line)?
• If you start to lose your balance, what kinds of things do you do with your body?
• Does holding your arms out or moving your body around help you stay on the beam (curb/line) a little bit better? Why?

This is why:
When you start to lose your balance, you try to regain it by bending and twisting your body, or by holding your arms out. In order to remain balanced, you must have the same amount of weight on each side of your body. By moving around, you are trying to equalize the weight on each side of your body.

Activity 2

For each small group, you will need:
a ruler
a rectangular rubber eraser

What to do:
Have youngsters in each group take turns trying to balance the ruler on the eraser.

Questions to ask:
• Where do you need to place the eraser in order to balance the ruler on it? Why?
• What happens if you move the eraser toward one end of the ruler? Why?

This is why:
The point of balance on the ruler is in the middle. The eraser has to be placed in the middle of the ruler so that there is as much weight on one side as there is on the other.

Thinking:
• How does this activity relate to walking on the balance beam (curb/line)?

Pam Crane

Activity 3

For each small group, you will need:
a ruler
a rectangular rubber eraser (or suitable substitute)
ten pennies

What to do:

Have each group balance the ruler on the eraser as described in Activity 2. Then ask each group to place a penny on one end of the balanced ruler. Have each group move the eraser in order to balance the ruler again (while the penny remains on the ruler).

Questions to ask:

• What happens when you place a penny on one end of the ruler? Why?
• What do you need to do to get the ruler balanced again? Why?

This is why:

Placing a penny on one end of the ruler adds weight to that end of the ruler. Because the weight is no longer equal on each side, the point of balance changes. The new point of balance is closer to the end with the penny, so the eraser has to be moved in that direction.

Free exploration:

Have each group continue to experiment by adding and subtracting pennies on the ruler as they wish. Encourage each group to move the eraser to find the new point of balance each time the ruler becomes unbalanced.

Activity 4

For each small group, you will need:
rulers/yardsticks

What to do:

In turn have each child rest the ends of a ruler (or yardstick) on his index fingers as shown. Then have him slowly slide one finger toward the center of the ruler, leaving his other finger and hand still.

Questions to ask:

• What happens when you slide your finger toward the center of the ruler?
• Were you able to move one finger without anything else moving? Why not?

This is why:

The ruler's point of balance is right in the middle of it. As you slowly move one finger toward the center of the ruler, it begins to tip slightly toward that finger. As it tips toward the moving finger, the weight on the other end of the ruler is reduced. The light end of the ruler begins to slide over the other finger until both fingers are in the middle and the ruler is balanced.

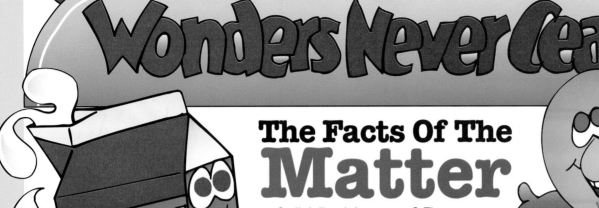

Wonders Never Cease

The Facts Of The Matter

Solid, liquid, or gas? These activities will have your youngsters eager to get right down to the facts of matter!

Activity 1

For each small group, you will need:
samples of matter
    solids: a book, a ruler, a block
    liquids: milk, juice, water
    gasses: an inflated balloon, a sealed Ziploc® bag

What to do:
    For each small group, place all of the materials on a table or the floor. Encourage youngsters to examine each of the items.

Questions to ask:
- How are the items alike?
- How are the items different?
- Which items take up space?
- Which items have weight?
- Are all of the items books? Juice?
- What could all of these items be called?

Explanation:
    All of the items are forms of matter. *Matter is anything that takes up space and has weight. Every material we know of is a form of matter.*

Thinking:
- Name some other things that are matter.
- Can you think of anything that is not matter? *(thoughts, feelings, dreams, shadows)*

Activity 2

For each small group, you will need:
wooden blocks
a bowl
a ruler

What to do:
    Direct each group to examine the blocks.

Questions to ask:
- Can the blocks be seen easily?
- What shapes are they?
- Can you easily change their shapes?
- Do the blocks take up space and have weight?

Then:
    Have each group place some of the blocks in the bowl. Then have youngsters move other blocks from place to place in your classroom. Also ask each group to try to move a ruler through the blocks.

Questions to ask:
- Did the blocks change their shapes when you put them in the bowl?
- Did the blocks change their shapes when you moved them from place to place? Why not?
- Could you move a ruler through the blocks? Why not?

This is why:
    A block is a form of solid *matter. Most solids can be easily seen and keep their shapes no matter where you place them. Most solids do not allow a solid object to be moved through them easily.*

Just for fun:
    Have youngsters explore your classroom, the schoolyard, and their homes to gather a collection of items that meet the criteria for solid matter.

Pam Crane

Activity 3

For each small group, you will need:

a cup of water a ruler
a resealable plastic bag a bowl
a jar

What to do:

Assist each group in pouring the cup of water into the plastic bag. After squeezing most of the air out of the bag, seal the bag. Direct each group to gently move and squeeze the bag; then lay the bag on a flat surface.

Questions to ask:

- What do you see in the bag?
- Does it change its shape easily?
- Does it take up space and have weight?

Then:

Have each group pour the water into the jar and examine it. Encourage each group member to try to move a ruler through the water. Then direct each group to pour the water into the bowl.

Questions to ask:

- Did its shape change when the water was in the jar and/or the bowl? Why?
- Could you move a ruler through the water? Why?

This is why:

Water is a liquid form of matter. Most liquids can be seen and change shape easily. A liquid takes on the shape of the container it is in. Liquids do allow solid objects to pass through them easily.

Just for fun:

Have youngsters explore your classroom and their homes and dictate as you write a list of as many liquids as they can think of. When the list is complete, challenge youngsters to take one day to think of just one more liquid!

Activity 4

For each small group, you will need:

a resealable plastic bag a glass
a ruler

What to do:

Have one child in each group blow into the bag; then quickly zip it shut. Encourage each member of the group to gently manipulate and squeeze the bag. Next have each group place the bag in different places such as resting on a flat surface or inside a glass. Then have each group open the bag and move a ruler through the air inside the bag.

Questions to ask:

- Can you see anything in the bag? Why not?
- Is there something in the bag? How can you tell?
- Does it change its shape easily?
- Does it have weight? (This concept may require more discussion. If desired, weigh two inflated balloons on a scale or balance. Then deflate one of the balloons and reweigh each balloon. Discuss the results.)
- Can you move a ruler through the air? Why?

This is why:

Air is in the bag. Air is a form of matter that is a gas. Most gasses cannot be seen. They change shape very easily and do allow solid objects to move through them easily.

Wonders Never Cease

Science For Early Childhood Teachers

Winter's Frozen Magic

Winter is filled with unique opportunities for scientific learning. So gather your supplies and use these suggestions to teach your youngsters about snowflakes, icicles, frost, frozen water, and melting snow.

ideas by Margie Dunlevy

Activity 1
Snowflakes

You will need:

a snowy day
a freezer
a 4" x 6" sheet of black construction paper
  for each student
magnifying glasses (one per student, if possible)

What to do:

On a snowy day, place construction-paper sheets in the freezer. When the paper is cold, have each student take a sheet of paper and a magnifying glass outside and attempt to catch two snowflakes on the paper. Using magnifying glasses, have students examine the snowflakes on their papers.

Questions to ask:

• How many sides or points do snowflakes have?
• Do your snowflakes look alike?
• How do you think snowflakes are made?
• What would happen to your snowflakes if you carried them inside? Why?

This is why:

All snow crystals have six sides and are either flat and platelike or long and columnar in shape.
No two snowflakes are alike. It is believed to be impossible for two snowflakes to be identical because they would have to fall through exactly the same air temperature and moisture levels on their way to Earth in order to be the same. This is highly unlikely. But in 1988 one physicist, Nancy Wright, caught two seemingly identical snowflakes. Examining enlarged photos of the snowflakes revealed no difference. Ms. Wright believes the differences may be so slight that we can't see them.
Clouds with temperatures below freezing contain microscopic particles. When water vapor attaches itself to one of these microscopic particles, a snow crystal forms.
If a snowflake crystal gets warm, it melts, and there is nothing left but a drop of water.

Activity 2
Icicles

You will need:

a 32° or colder day
a coffee can   string
a hammer   water
a nail   food coloring

What to do:

In advance, use the hammer and nail to punch three holes near the top of a coffee can and one small hole in the bottom. Thread a length of string through the holes near the top of the can, and tie all three remaining string ends together. On a freezing or below-freezing day, have youngsters fill the can with water and tint the water with food coloring. Have youngsters assist in suspending the can from a tree branch overnight. Have youngsters discuss the results the following day.

Questions to ask:

• What do you see?
• How did this happen?
• What is the name for this formation?
• What will happen to this formation if it gets warmer?

This is why:

One by one drops of water escape from the hole in the bottom of the can. These drops freeze onto the cold can bottom. As more drops come out, they freeze atop the frozen water drops, forming an icicle.

Pam Crane

Activity 3
Frost

You will need:
crushed ice
a coffee can   paper
salt   a spoon
1/2 tsp. water   magnifying glasses

What to do:
Have youngsters fill a coffee can 2/3 full of crushed ice. Fill the remainder of the can with salt, and gently stir. Have a youngster put 1/2 tsp. of water on a sheet of paper, smooth it into a thin layer, and set the can on top of the paper. Have students observe the icy formations using magnifying glasses.

Questions to ask:
• What happened? What does it look like?
• Where have you seen this kind of icy formation before?
• What happened to the wet paper under the can? Why?

This is why:
Adding salt lowered the temperature of the ice. Moist air came in contact with the cold can. The moisture froze and stuck to the can. This frozen moisture is called frost. This experiment shows that a gas (water vapor) can be changed into a solid (frost). The moisture on the wet paper beneath the can froze in the same manner, perhaps sticking it to the can.

Activity 4
Water Gets Bigger

You will need:
a plastic soft-drink bottle
a freezer   aluminum foil
water

What to do:
Have youngsters fill a plastic bottle to the top with water. Place a loosely fitting aluminum-foil cap on the bottle. Freeze the bottle overnight. Have your youngsters observe the changes.

Questions to ask:
• What happened to the water?
• Why did this happen?
• Since water gets bigger as it freezes, what problems could this cause?

This is why:
Most substances contract as they get colder. But, as it freezes, water expands. Because of this characteristic, expanding water—or freezing water—can break water pipes in and around our homes.

Activity 5
Meltdown

You will need:
snow
a large bowl
a coffee filter

What to do:
Have youngsters fill the bowl to the rim with snow and set it in your classroom. Several hours later, have youngsters observe the changes in the bowl. After asking your youngsters the first two questions below, pour the water from the bowl through a coffee filter.

Questions to ask:
• What happened to the snow?
• Why isn't the bowl full of water?
• Did the filter catch anything?
• If so, how did it get in the snow?

This is why:
A great deal of air was trapped between the snowflakes in the bowl. In addition to that, an identical amount of moisture takes up more space when frozen. So, as the snow melted and the moisture temperature increased, the water molecules contracted and the air that was trapped between snowflakes escaped. Therefore the resulting pool of water looks small in contrast to its equivalent of snow.
Debris in the melted snow is either natural or man-made. Natural pollution, which helps clouds form and rain fall, includes volcanic ash, pollen, tiny plant bits, and ocean salt. Man-made pollution, which is dangerous to our health and to our planet, comes from our cars, furnaces, machinery, and factories.

Cooling Off And Warming Up

Introduce your youngsters to the thermometer.

Important Note: Activities 1 and 2 must be done in rapid succession.

For the activities on this page, you will need:

a thermos of ice-cold water that has been tinted with red food coloring

a thermos of lukewarm water that has been tinted with yellow food coloring

a thermos of very warm water that has been tinted with blue food coloring (Test this water to be certain that it is significantly warmer than the lukewarm water but not warm enough to be uncomfortable to the touch or to burn the skin.)

three baby-food jars for each small group of children

paper towels

copies of the record sheet on page 46

pencils

Preparing for the experiment:

Divide the youngsters into small groups with an adult or older student assigned to each group. Place three baby-food jars, paper towels, a pencil, and a record sheet (page 46) on a tabletop in front of each group.

Pam Crane

Activity 1

What to do:

For each group, fill one of the jars with red water and one with yellow water. Have each child in turn hold a finger in the red water for ten seconds. Then have him remove his finger from the red water and hold it in the yellow water. In the space provided on the record sheet, have the adult or older student record the child's description of the yellow water's temperature while his finger is in the water.

Questions to ask:
• How did the red water feel?
• How did the yellow water feel?

Activity 2

What to do:

Fill each group's third jar with the blue water. (Test it again to be certain it is significantly warmer than the yellow water but not warm enough to be uncomfortable to the touch or to burn.) Have each youngster in turn hold a finger in the blue water for up to ten seconds. Then have him move the finger to the yellow water. In the space provided on the record sheet, have the adult or older student record the child's description of the yellow water's temperature while his finger is in the water.

Questions to ask:
• How did the blue water feel?
• How did the yellow water feel?

This is why:

The red water was cold. Because the yellow water felt warmer than the red water, youngsters probably described it as warm.

This is why:

Since the blue water was significantly warmer than the yellow water, students will probably describe the yellow water as being cool.

Activity 4

You will need:
a collection of thermometers
a collection of other instruments of measure
 (such as scales, rulers, and calendars)
a cloth to cover the instruments

What to do:
   Place your collection of thermometers and other instruments of measure on a tabletop when youngsters aren't looking. Cover the instruments with the cloth.

Questions to ask:
• What are we measuring if we want to know how warm or cool something is?
• Since we've seen that our bodies can become confused about how warm or cool something is, how can we really know what the correct temperature actually is?
• What is the name of an instrument that measures how hot or cold something is?

What to do:
   Uncover your collection, and ask student volunteers to take turns explaining the purpose of each instrument. Then have them locate all the instruments that measure temperature. Have youngsters place thermometers at different indoor and outdoor locations. On a daily basis, assist youngsters as they check the thermometers and compare the temperatures.

Activity 3

What to do:
   Collect the record sheets. Share some of the responses from Activity One with youngsters. Then share some of the responses from Activity Two.

Questions to ask:
• What color was the water you described in Activity One?
• What color was the water you described in Activity Two?
• Was it the same water?
• Did you think it felt the same both times that you touched it?
• Why did you describe it differently if it was the same water?

This is why:

   Your brain receives signals from your skin. In Activity One, your brain got signals from your skin that indicated that the yellow water was warm in contrast to the red water. In Activity Two, your brain received signals that indicated the yellow water was cool in contrast to the blue water. But since the yellow water was about the same in temperature both times, this means your body reached conflicting conclusions about the yellow water.

   Field crickets are known as the "poor man's thermometers." Count the number of chirps in a 15-second period; then add 37 to it. The number you get will usually be very close to the actual Fahrenheit temperature.

   After sharing this amazing information with your youngsters, read aloud Eric Carle's The Very Quiet Cricket. Just for fun, time and count the chirps and figure the temperature according to the "cricket" in the book.

45

Cooling Off And Warming Up
Record Sheet

Activity 1   How did the yellow water feel?

Activity 2   How did the yellow water feel?

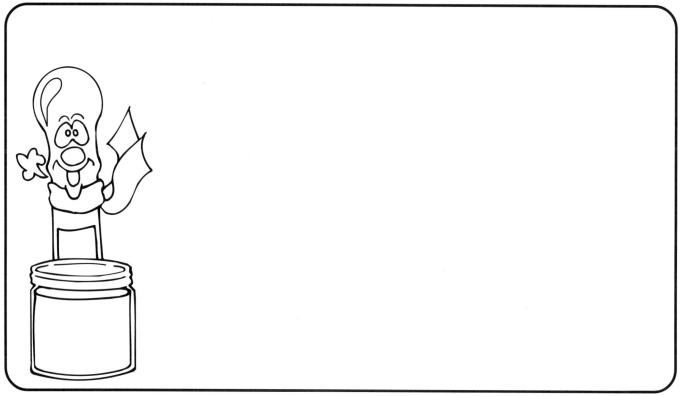

Note To The Teacher: Use with Activities 1–3 on pages 44–45.

Wonders Never Cease

Science For Early Childhood Teachers

"Polar" Attractions

Set forth on a polar expedition! With this collection of "attractive" hands-on activities, youngsters can explore the secrets of magnets and magnetism.

Activity 1

You will need:
an assortment of magnets

What to do:
Divide youngsters into groups. Give each group an assortment of magnets. Allow time for exploration and discovery.

Questions to ask:
- What shapes are the magnets?
- Where have you seen magnets?
- Why do people use magnets?

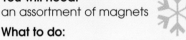

This is why:
Magnets come in all shapes and sizes. Some magnets are horseshoe shaped. Others are round or rectangular. Magnets can be found on magnetic memo holders, magnetic letters and numbers, and on the insides of refrigerator doors. Magnets have many uses including holding doors closed, helping computers to "remember" information, and helping radio and television speakers create sounds.

Pam Crane

Activity 2

You will need:
two bar magnets
two paper clips
a construction-paper copy of the polar bear and sled pattern (page 49)

What to do:
Color and cut out the pattern. Cut apart the polar bear and the sled. Laminate the cutouts for durability if desired. Bend the paper clips at 90° angles. Tape one paper clip to the back of the bear cutout and the other to the back of the sled cutout. Position the magnets so that like poles are facing one another. Place the cutouts atop the magnets. Have youngsters attempt to push the magnets together.

Stop and ask:
- Why can't the polar bear get his sled?

Then:
Reposition the magnets so that opposite poles are facing one another; then reposition the cutouts. Have youngsters slide the magnets closer and closer together until the magnets attract one another.

Questions to ask:
- What happened the first time we tried to push the magnets together?
- Why do you think this happened?
- What happened the second time we tried to push the magnets together?
- Why do you think this happened?

This is why:
Each magnet has a north pole (end) and a south pole (end). During the first attempt, the magnets repelled or pushed one another away because like poles (north and north or south and south) were placed together. The second time, the magnets were attracted or pulled together because unlike poles (north and south) were placed together.

Activity 3

You will need:
an assortment of magnetic and nonmagnetic objects (ten objects per group)
red paper plates (one per group)
green paper plates (one per group)
magnetic tape (a one-inch strip for each child)
construction-paper polar bears (pattern page 49 (one per child))

What to do:
Have each child color and cut out his pattern, then attach his magnetic tape to his polar bear's paw. Divide youngsters into groups. Place an assortment of items in the center of each group along with a green and a red paper plate. Using the magnetic tape strip on his cutout, have each youngster test each object to determine whether or not it is attracted to the strip. Then have youngsters place each object that was attracted to the strip on the green plate and each object that was not attracted on the red plate.

Questions to ask:
- How are all of the items that were attracted to the magnet alike?
- What types of things are attracted to magnets?
- Why do you think the items on your red plate were not attracted to the magnetic strip?

This is why:
The items that were attracted to the magnetic tape are all made of metal. Most (or all) of them are shiny. Things made of iron, steel, nickel, or cobalt are attracted to a magnet. The items on the red plate were not made of iron, steel, nickel, or cobalt.

Activity 4

You will need:
objects attracted to a magnet
(from Activity 3)
paper clips (two per child)
clear plastic cups (one per child)
water
several bar magnets

What to do:
Have each youngster place an object that was attracted to a magnet (from Activity 3) and two paper clips in a clear plastic cup. Then have him fill his cup halfway with water. Have each youngster place a magnet on the side of his cup and slowly move it around the outside surface.

Questions to ask:
• How were you able to move the objects in the water?
• Why did the objects move toward the magnet?

This is why:
The objects in the water were moved with a magnet. Magnetic forces can travel through water and plastic. So, even though the objects were in a plastic cup filled with water, they were still attracted to the magnet.

Activity 5

You will need:
polar bear cutouts (from
Activity 3)
paper clips (one per child)
tape
bar magnets (one per group)
wooden rulers (one per group)
paper plates (one per child)
blue tempera paint (optional)

What to do:
Tape each bar magnet to one end of a ruler. Assist each child in bending his paper clip into a 90° angle and taping it to the back of his cutout. To make his cutout "skate," a youngster has a partner hold a paper plate. He then places his cutout atop the paper plate. Next, using the ruler as a handle, he places the magnet under the paper plate, then manipulates the ruler to move the cutout. For a colorful variation, have each youngster put a dab of paint in the center of his plate before manipulating his cutout with the magnet.

Questions to ask:
• What made your polar bear "skate"?
• Would the polar bear have skated without the paper clip attached? Why or why not?

This is why:
Through the paper plate, the magnet attracted the paper clip. Without the paper clip attached to it, the cutout would not have been attracted to the magnet.

Activity 6

You will need:
paper plates (one per child)
several round magnets
iron filings (or fine-gauge steel wool
cut into tiny pieces)
several plastic spoons
spray fixative
scissors
monofilament line

What to do:
Place several magnets on a tabletop. In turn, have each youngster place his paper plate atop a magnet, then use a plastic spoon to sprinkle iron filings on top of his plate. Spray the plate with several light coats of fixative, letting the project dry between coats. Remove the magnet. To create a "snowflake," have each youngster cut loosely around his design. Suspend each youngster's project from the ceiling using monofilament line for an "attractive" display.

Questions to ask:
• How would you describe the shape of the filings on your plate?
• Why did the filings line up this way?

This is why:
The iron filings collected in patterns. The patterns illustrate the magnetic field of the magnet.

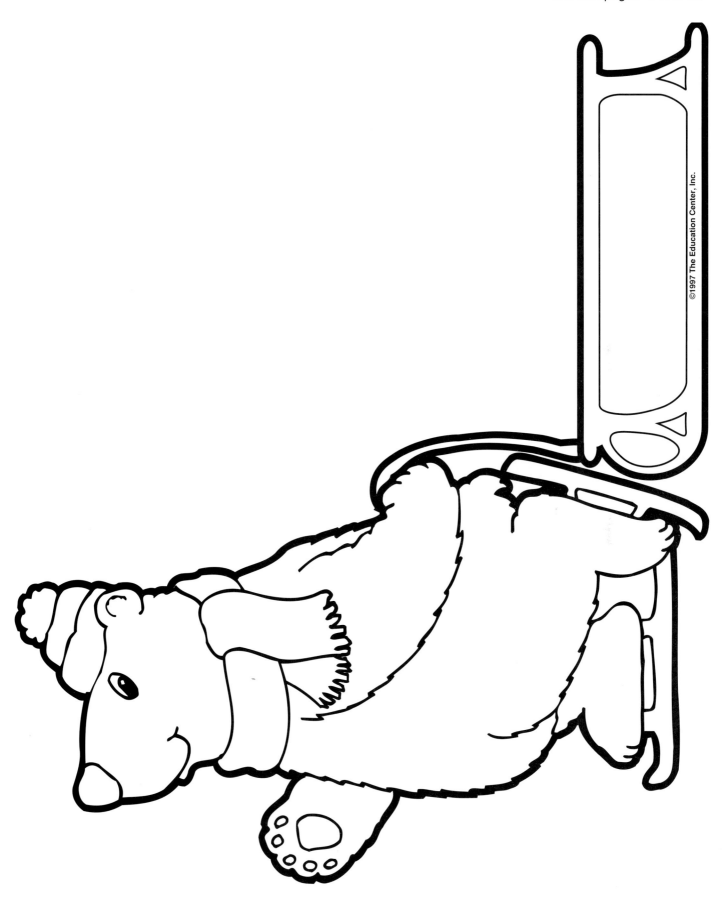

©1997 The Education Center, Inc.

Shopping Savvy Booklet

Begin this activity by asking youngsters to generate a list of foods from each of the six groups in the food pyramid. Discuss which of these foods would be smart choices for good nutrition. Then use the booklet patterns on pages 58–60 to provide youngsters with an opportunity to create their own grocery lists. Duplicate one copy of the booklet cover (page 58) onto construction paper for each child. Then duplicate five copies of the shopping list booklet page (page 59). Program the first line on each of these shopping list pages with the name of a food group. Then duplicate one copy of each page for each child. Also duplicate the last booklet page (page 60) for each child. Compile each child's seven pages together and staple them along the left edge.

Have each child personalize and color his booklet cover. Then encourage youngsters to draw one or more appropriate food items on each shopping list page. Write as students dictate the name of each illustrated food item. Lastly have each child write or draw to complete the last page of the booklet. Present each nutritious food shopper with a personalized copy of the award on page 57.

Fantastic Foods

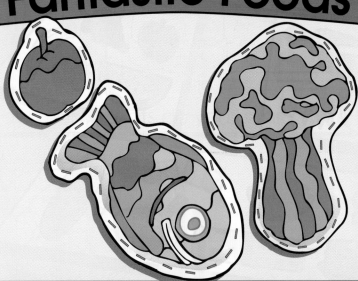

Fantastic Foods

This giant-sized art display will inspire good nutrition schoolwide and win big compliments for your youngsters. Provide children with large sheets of white bulletin-board paper, a variety of colors of tempera paints, and paintbrushes. Encourage each child to paint giant-sized fruits, vegetables, breads, meats, and dairy products. When the paintings are dry, cut out each one. Place each cutout on a sheet of bulletin-board paper and trace its shape. Cut on each resulting outline. Staple each painted shape atop its plain match, leaving a few inches unstapled. Stuff each resulting food shape with crumpled newspaper or plastic grocery bags; then staple it shut. Display these enormously tempting food items on a wall in the hallway with the title "Fantastic Foods."

Cooperative Bulletin Board

Making this bulletin board will reinforce good nutrition concepts as well as providing an attractive nutrition reminder for the days ahead. In advance, prepare 21 paper plates. Cut out construction-paper circles (each one sized to cover the center of a plate) in the following colors and amounts: 6 tan, 5 green, 4 red, 3 white, 2 brown, 1 yellow. Glue each circle to the center of a different plate. Then divide youngsters into groups. Assign each group of children a specific food group. Give each group its plates accordingly as follows: breads=tan, vegetables=green, fruits=red, dairy=white, meats=brown, and fats/sweets=yellow. Have children look through magazines to identify and cut out pictures that fit into their designated food groups. Then instruct each group to glue one picture on each paper plate. When the pictures are secured, enlist the help of your youngsters to arrange the plates in the appropriate food pyramid shape (as shown). Write the name of each food group on a sentence strip and post it near its matching row of plates.

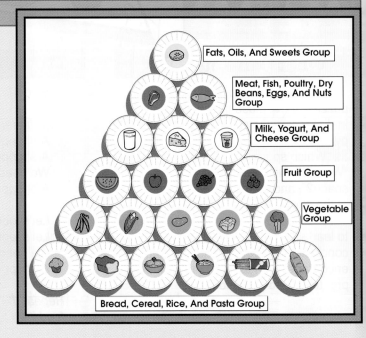

Grocery Bag Sorting

Reinforce your youngsters' classification skills with this simple sorting activity. Gather a wide variety of toy foods and clean, empty food containers. (Be sure that cans have no sharp edges.) Tape all boxes shut, and stuff empty food bags with newspaper before stapling them closed. Store these food containers in colorful milk crates. Provide one large paper grocery bag for each of the six food groups, and label and illustrate each bag. To do this activity, a youngster takes the food packages from the crates and sorts them into the appropriate grocery bags.

Fun-With-Food Books

Create a motivating reading center with a collection of books (see the "Food Book Bibliography"), a toy grocery cart, a colorful shopping bag, and a chalkboard slate. Write "Today's Special" on the slate and place the book of your choice in the bag. At storytime, take that day's book out of the bag to share with your little ones. After you read the book, store it in the shopping cart for youngsters to enjoy during their free time.

Nutritious Nibbling

After all this talk about nutrition, don't you think it's only fitting to experience the reality of it all? Take some time to survey your children to find out what their favorite food items are in each food group. Extend this survey into a graphing activity if desired. Then select some of the favorite foods mentioned in each food group and serve them on paper plates arranged in a pyramid shape.

Food Book Bibliography

Eating Fractions
Written & Photographed by Bruce McMillan
Published by Scholastic Inc.

Potluck
Written by Anne Shelby
Illustrated by Irene Trivas
Published by Orchard Books

Stone Soup
Written & Illustrated by Marcia Brown
Published by Aladdin

The Very Hungry Caterpillar
Written & Illustrated by Eric Carle
Published by Scholastic Inc.

What Food Is This?
Written & Photographed by Rosmarie Hausherr
Published by Scholastic Inc.

Gregory, The Terrible Eater
Written by Mitchell Sharmat
Illustrated by Jose Aruego and Ariane Dewey
Published by Scholastic Inc.

Grandpa's Garden Lunch
Written & Illustrated by Judith Caseley
Published by Greenwillow Books

Eat Up, Gemma
Written by Sarah Hayes
Illustrated by Jan Ormerod
Published by Lothrop, Lee & Shepard Books

What's For Lunch?
Written by John Schindel
Illustrated by Kevin O'Malley
Published by Lothrop, Lee & Shepard Books

Patterns

Use with "Food Pyramid Puzzle"
on page 53.

THE SUPER SHOPPER AWARD

goes to _____

for choosing healthy foods!

Dear Parent,

   We have been studying nutrition at school. Please ask your child to tell you what we have learned about good-for-you foods!

MILK

My Healthy Shopping List

by

My shopping list for _____

Yogurt

I can shop for healthy foods.

My favorite grain food is _____ .

My favorite fruit is _____ .

My favorite vegetable is _____ .

My favorite dairy food is _____ .

My favorite protein food is _____ .

Getting In Tune With Your Senses
Featuring
The Fab Five

Welcome, ladies and gentlemen, to the opening performance of The Fab Five. Awesome crowd! Before the show begins, I'd like to take this opportunity to thank all our classroom-teacher fans for keeping that fan mail coming. Way to go. Absolutely! We've noted your special requests and dedications and worked as many of them as possible into our totally tubular five-senses show. So without further ado, dude, let's give a hearty welcome to THE FAB FIVE!

I Know That Voice

If you really want students to have a blast while they exercise their sense of hearing, then this idea is the one for you! First videotape several different cartoons or obtain several cartoon videotapes featuring different cartoon characters. Then use a cassette recorder to make an audiotape of snippets of the dialogues from the videotapes, orally assigning each snippet a different number. As you tape each bit of conversation, note the cartoon character who said it. Later replay the audiotape for your youngsters. Have students guess each cartoon character's identity; then check their responses by referring to your notes. Afterward place the tape in a listening station with a numbered picture answer key, and encourage youngsters to use the tape independently.

Mary Sutula—Preschool
Orlando, FL

Hello, Friend

Few sounds are sweeter than the sounds of a familiar voice. So play this hearing-related guessing game to get your youngsters to use their sense of hearing. Have one child sit near the front of the room, facing away from his classmates. Silently select three other students to address the student seated at the front of the room. Ask each of these three students, in turn, to say, "Hello, [insert first student's name]." After the three youngsters have greeted him, have the student who was greeted name the students who spoke to him. If the listener makes at least one correct guess, have the first person he correctly identifies take his place. If not, select one of the students who spoke to take his place. If you're using this game during a holiday period, have students give a holiday greeting rather than just a simple, "Hello."

Mary Sutula—Preschool

What Was That?

Here's a way to help students concentrate on using their sense of hearing to identify typically unnoticed noises. Make an audio-tape of various distinctive household and classroom sounds. Tape ordinary sounds such as running water, tearing paper, and filling a glass with ice and water. Make notes so that you can be sure of the origin of each sound that you tape. Then play the sounds one at a time for your youngsters to identify. To use this tape in a listening center, include a picture card for each sound. Have students listen to the tape and point to the picture that relates to the sound.

M. Carroll, Jacksonville, FL

Sounds Like Fun!

Give your students' ears a workout by creating this game that starts with something you might have an abundance of—crayon boxes. For this activity, you will need an even number of empty crayon boxes. Identically fill pairs of boxes with different items such as toothpicks, pennies, sand, or tacks. Seal each box and cover it with Con-Tact® covering. For self-checking, put identical stickers on the bottoms of each pair of boxes with the same contents. To use this activity, have a student shake the boxes in an effort to find the box pairs that make the same sound. Once he has decided which boxes match, have the student flip the boxes to check his responses.

Jane Chastain—Gr. K, Holly Springs Elementary School, Pickens, SC

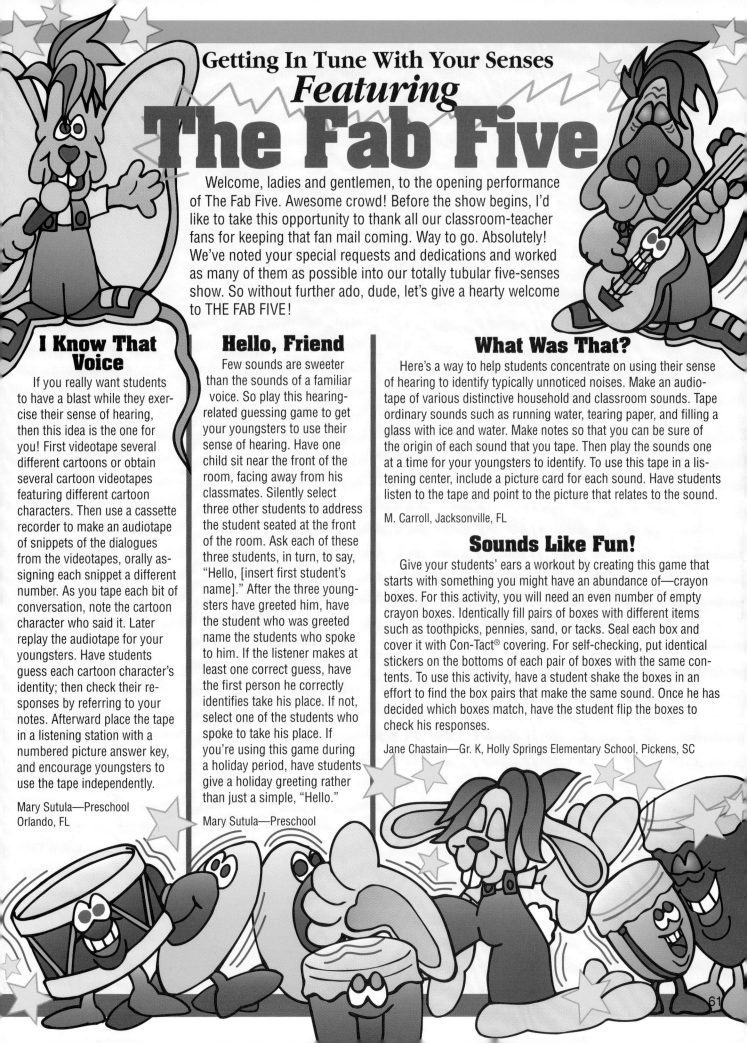

"Touch Me" Book

Youngsters won't want to take their hands off these books. Begin this project by asking each youngster to contribute 2" x 4" rectangles of various textured materials to be made into a book. Provide additional textured samples. Once your collection of textures is complete, have each youngster incorporate several into a booklet. Encourage each child to share his booklet with others and describe each of the textures it contains.

Doris Russell, Sun Prairie, WI

Textures Around Us

Challenge your little ones to investigate the textures in the natural world around them. Divide your students into small groups and have them walk around your campus. Encourage students to find something that looks as though it would have an interesting texture or feel. Before permitting them to touch the selected item, photograph the group members with the item and ask them to predict how it will feel. Then encourage each group member to touch and describe the texture of the object. Note each group's description. Find out whether or not students' predictions were accurate. When the pictures have been developed, glue each one into a blank booklet and write the youngsters' descriptions beneath the picture.

Sheli Gossett, Sebring, FL

Screening

With this idea, the sense of touch is the focal point both during the process and, inherently, in the result. In preparation for this activity, staple a piece of screen to an identically sized piece of cardboard. Then use wide tape to tape the screen securely to the cardboard. Provide a supply of crayons and paper for students to use with the screen. Encourage each youngster to bear down a little more than normal as he takes a turn writing or drawing on a sheet of paper placed on top of the screen. Once the child has done this, have him feel the texture of his work and comment on how it feels to the touch.

Ariela L. Mahoney—Gr. K
Mitchell School
Needham, MA

It's In The Bag

Using his sense of touch, each youngster can match an unseen item to the picture ca that corresponds to it. Make few small cloth bags or use c socks for this purpose. Colle some small household items that will fit into the bags or socks you will use. Make a pi ture card to represent each item; then place each item in bag (or sock) and stitch (or t the opening. Place the cards and the bags in a center. Hav students take turns feeling th objects inside the bags and matching each bag to a picture.

Jane Chastain—Gr. K
Holly Springs Elementary Schoo
Pickens, SC

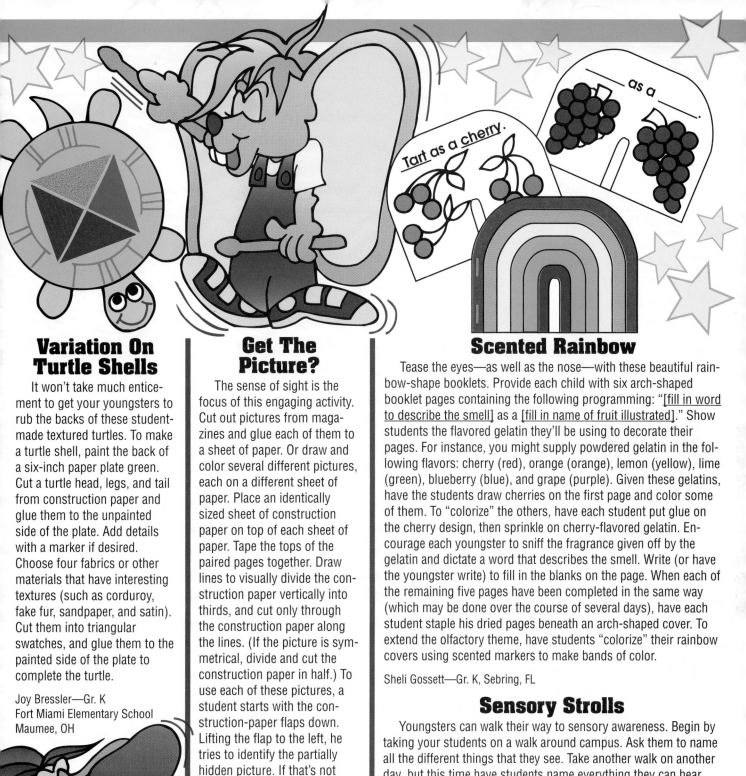

Variation On Turtle Shells

It won't take much enticement to get your youngsters to rub the backs of these student-made textured turtles. To make a turtle shell, paint the back of a six-inch paper plate green. Cut a turtle head, legs, and tail from construction paper and glue them to the unpainted side of the plate. Add details with a marker if desired. Choose four fabrics or other materials that have interesting textures (such as corduroy, fake fur, sandpaper, and satin). Cut them into triangular swatches, and glue them to the painted side of the plate to complete the turtle.

Joy Bressler—Gr. K
Fort Miami Elementary School
Maumee, OH

Get The Picture?

The sense of sight is the focus of this engaging activity. Cut out pictures from magazines and glue each of them to a sheet of paper. Or draw and color several different pictures, each on a different sheet of paper. Place an identically sized sheet of construction paper on top of each sheet of paper. Tape the tops of the paired pages together. Draw lines to visually divide the construction paper vertically into thirds, and cut only through the construction paper along the lines. (If the picture is symmetrical, divide and cut the construction paper in half.) To use each of these pictures, a student starts with the construction-paper flaps down. Lifting the flap to the left, he tries to identify the partially hidden picture. If that's not enough information, he lifts the next flap on the left. Finally he lifts the last flap to reveal the picture or to confirm his guess.

Virginia Chaverri—Gr. Pre/K

Scented Rainbow

Tease the eyes—as well as the nose—with these beautiful rainbow-shape booklets. Provide each child with six arch-shaped booklet pages containing the following programming: "[fill in word to describe the smell] as a [fill in name of fruit illustrated]." Show students the flavored gelatin they'll be using to decorate their pages. For instance, you might supply powdered gelatin in the following flavors: cherry (red), orange (orange), lemon (yellow), lime (green), blueberry (blue), and grape (purple). Given these gelatins, have the students draw cherries on the first page and color some of them. To "colorize" the others, have each student put glue on the cherry design, then sprinkle on cherry-flavored gelatin. Encourage each youngster to sniff the fragrance given off by the gelatin and dictate a word that describes the smell. Write (or have the youngster write) to fill in the blanks on the page. When each of the remaining five pages have been completed in the same way (which may be done over the course of several days), have each student staple his dried pages beneath an arch-shaped cover. To extend the olfactory theme, have students "colorize" their rainbow covers using scented markers to make bands of color.

Sheli Gossett—Gr. K, Sebring, FL

Sensory Strolls

Youngsters can walk their way to sensory awareness. Begin by taking your students on a walk around campus. Ask them to name all the different things that they see. Take another walk on another day, but this time have students name everything they can hear. On subsequent days, have students take other walks specifically to explore their senses of touch and smell. To explore students' sense of taste, pack some bite-size treats that are sweet (fruit candy), sour (pickles), salty (pretzels), and bitter (bittersweet chocolate), and take them along on a walk. Pause to picnic on the treats and discuss the differences in the tastes.

Cara Schlotter—Preschool, Faith Christian Child Care, Washington, IL

Pam Crane

Interactive Display

Near the conclusion of your unit on the five senses, get students involved in creating collages and interactive displays that represent the senses. Have students work in small groups to create five collages, each of which features one of these body parts: eyes, ears, noses, hands, or mouths. Display each of the collages, and set up a companion display nearby that is indicative of the sense being depicted. For example, in front of the eyes collage could be a display containing glasses, goggles, a microscope, binoculars, mirrors, and magnifying glasses. Musical instruments, different sizes of bells, books with musical or sound effects, a cassette player, and a recording of environmental sounds could be arranged in front of the ears collage. And cotton balls scented with peppermint, cloves, cinnamon, vinegar, and onions could be placed in front of the nose collage, along with fragrant flowers and perfumes. Add interest in front of the hands collage by accompanying it with a "feely box" and a banner with lots of different textures on it. Top off the mouth collage with food items such as lemon balls, pretzels, pickles, bittersweet chocolate, and something sweet. Then invite everyone to explore and enjoy.

Sandra Ziegler—Preschool, St. Mary's Catholic School, Strongsville, OH

Christine Wirtanen, Northeast, Evergreen Park, IL

Bread-Making Bonanza

Baking bread can be a sensory bonanza for your class. Prepare two loaves of dough for the oven before class, and begin baking them just before you and your students begin mixing the ingredients for another two loaves. Let the second batch of dough rise; then gather the children around to punch it down and take turns kneading it. While baking bread, youngsters can see how flour and yeast turn into a brown crusty loaf. They can feel the texture of the dough and the bread. They can smell the aroma of the baking bread and taste the flavor once it's done. And what will they hear? "Mmmmmm!"

Doris Russell, Sun Prairie, WI

Singing The Senses

Here's a song that will leave you with an earful—of a sensory song, that is.

(sung to the tune of "Bingo")

We use five senses every day
To help us learn and play.
See, hear, smell, touch, taste.
See, hear, smell, touch, taste.
See, hear, smell, touch, taste.
We do these every day.

Penni Flood—Pre/K
Park Village Elementary
San Antonio, TX

Literature Tie-Ins

Rachel Isadora's books about senses make marvelou conversation starters. Read aloud *I Hear, I See,* and *I Tou* (published by Greenwillow Books). As you read these books, pause to allow studen to say how they think the objects would feel, sound, or look. Follow up a reading of *I Touch* by giving students o portunities to feel around to discover what's in a "feely bo you've prepared for the occasion. After reading *I Hear,* giv each student rubber bands t stretch over an empty tissue box so that he may make a strummer for a parade. And off a reading of *I See* by hav each student use tempera pa mixed with glue to paint a cl plastic lid using lots of differ ent colors. Punch a hole in th lid, and thread the hole with yarn to make a sun catcher.

Karen Attanasio
Back Mountain Memorial Librar
Dallas, PA

A Trip Down Sensory Lane

Why not end your five-senses unit with a thematic flair? Using the descriptions below, set up a variety of specialty shops straight out of the early 1900s. Students will delight in visiting the unusual shops and testing out their senses. The end result—a culminating activity with sensory appeal!

- **Optical Review:** At this Wild West show, feature a clip from a 3-D movie or a collection of optical illusions.
- **Doctor Twin, M.D.:** For this shop enlist an eye-care professional to share information about eyes and proper eye care. An assortment of visual discrimination games could also be featured.
- **The Vibration Station:** Display an assortment of vibrating instruments such as tuning forks, guitars, and drums at this station. Students can stop by and fine-tune their hearing.
- **Firehouse Antics:** Students are all ears at the firehouse! Without revealing her sources, the Fire Chief (an adult volunteer) creates different sounds by tapping together and/or dropping a variety of unbreakable objects. Students try to identify how each sound is made.
- **The Perfumery:** Fill this shop with a collection of sniffing canisters and cutouts. To make a sniffing canister, dab a cotton ball with a desired scent and tuck the cotton ball inside an empty, plastic film canister. Punch a small hole in the canister's lid before snapping it in place. Then create a cutout that reveals the source of each smell (for example, a strawberry cutout for a strawberry scent and a vanilla bean cutout for a vanilla scent). Students sniff the canisters and match them to the appropriate cutouts.
- **The Sniff Smith:** At this shop, students find out how the sense of smell affects their sense of taste. Provide a sampling of unidentifiable foods. Students pinch their noses as they sample each food and try to determine its flavor. (To make foods unidentifiable, blend them in a food processor.)
- **The Tastery:** At this place of business, students use their taste buds to identify visually indistinguishable foods. Salt, white sugar, baking soda, and flour can be tasted. Or peel and dice raw apples, pears, and potatoes for sampling.
- **The Candy Shop:** Sweet (sugar), sour (lemon or pickle juice), bitter (powdered cocoa), and salty (salt) are tasted at this eatery. If desired, display a diagram that shows where each type of taste bud is found on the tongue.
- **The Feel Mercantile:** At this general store, each product is inside a burlap bag. Students try to determine what products are for sale by feeling the bags.
- **Rub-a-Dub Bathhouse:** Place several small items—such as erasers, pom-poms, golf balls, and plastic combs—in the bottom of a plastic tub or pool before filling the container with packing pellets. Students try to identify the objects under the pellets by touch. To check their hunches, they pull the objects to the surface.

Jean Wark—Gr. K, Perkins Elementary, St. Petersburg, FL

Water Play

Mix children, water, rocks, and scrub brushes. What have you got? You've got one great sensory experience! Place several large rocks of various textures and colors in the water table. Also include several sizes and types of scrub brushes and food coloring or liquid dish soap. Ask youngsters to scrub the rocks clean. The brushes will make interesting sounds; the rocks, dish soap, and food coloring will create interesting visual images; and the rocks, soap, and water all have fascinating textures to feel.

Susan Anker—Pre/K
Early Childhood Family Education
   Center
White Bear Lake, MN

Books About Senses

Sense Suspense: A Guessing Game For The Five Senses
Written & Photographed by Bruce McMillan
Published by Scholastic Inc.

My Five Senses
Written & Illustrated by Aliki
Published by HarperCollins Publishers

Senses All Around

Wrap up your study of the five senses with a sensory fair. Make plans to feature one or more center activities for each sense. (See the list of suggestions below.) In a parent note, explain the event and request needed supplies. Also enlist the help of several adult volunteers—at least one per center. To stage the event, arrange the adult-supervised center activities around the classroom. Then, under your direction, have students move from center to center along a predetermined route. Let's go to the fair!

Center suggestions:

- **Touch:** For this center, prepare one or more "feely boxes." To make a "feely box," remove the lid and cut an opening from each end of a shoebox. (A youngster must be able to slide one hand into each opening.) Fill the box with pairs of small items; then replace the box lid. A student slides his hands through the openings and feels the contents of the box. When the student thinks he's found two identical objects, he asks a parent volunteer or a classmate to remove the box lid so that he can check his work.

- **Hearing:** To make this center, you will need a supply of duplicated sound cards like the ones shown. A student arranges several cards in a row; then he performs the sounds in order by following the visual clues on his cards.

- **Sight:** Place a variety of optical devices—such as magnifying lenses, sunglasses, binoculars, and hand mirrors—at this exploration center. Once students have explored the optical apparatuses, the adult volunteer can engage students in a memory game in which the players try to determine which object the adult has removed from the collection.

- **Taste:** Slice or dice a variety of exotic fruits like mangoes, kiwifruits, papayas, passion fruits, and pineapple for this center. Display the fruit pieces and a supply of toothpicks. A student uses a toothpick to poke and sample a variety of fruits.

- **Smell:** For this center, place a different flavor of gelatin powder and/or ground spice in each of several small containers. A student sniffs the contents of each container in an effort to identify the corresponding smell. When all of the containers have been sniffed by a child or a group of children, the parent volunteer reveals the source of each smell. Next, on a sheet of drawing paper, each student illustrates one fruit or spice he smelled at the center. The parent volunteer uses double-sided tape to attach a sample of the corresponding powder to the student's completed project.

Doris Russell, Sun Prairie, WI

A Poppin' Good Time

Pop! Sniff! Crunch! Here's the perfect ending to a "sense-ational" unit! Under the watchful eyes of your youngsters, pop a sizable amount of popcorn kernels using an air popper. As the corn is popping, ask students to describe the sights, sounds, and smells of the popping corn. Also place a small container of popped and unpopped kernels at each table, and ask students to feel and describe the differences between the two forms of corn. Finally give each youngster a serving of popped corn and have him put his taste buds to the test. If desired, serve students small samplings of differently seasoned popcorn (such as salted, buttered, salted and buttered) and ask students to identify the different tastes; then record your youngsters' popcorn preferences on a class graph. Now that's wrapping up a unit in good taste!

Tina Nowakowski—Gr. K
East End Elementary
Humboldt, TN

What A Sight!

Take an insightful look at our sense of sight with Ed Young's delightful book *Seven Blind Mice* (published by Philomel Books). As the story unfolds, each of six colorful mice sizes up an unidentified object with different results. It's not until the seventh mouse sizes up the whole object that its true identity is revealed. To prepare a fun lead-in activity the story, cut several pictures of large objects from discarded magazines. Snip each object half. Display one part of each picture on the chalkboard and set aside the remaining cutouts for later use. To begin the activity, ask students to study the partial pictures on display and suggest what each object could be. List the students' predictions below the appropriate pictures. Take a moment discuss what makes this activity challenging; then read aloud the insightful mice tale. At the conclusion of the story, use the cutouts that were previously set aside to piece together the pictures on display. Much like the mice in the story, students are sure to conclude that our sense of sight is most valuable when we take the time to view things in their entirety.

Kathy Curnow—Gr. K
Woolridge Elementary
Midlothian, VA

Wonders Never Cease

Some "Sound" Ideas!

Shake, rattle, and roll with these hands-on science activities that will help your youngsters learn about sound.

by Marie Iannetti

Activity 1

You will need:
a ruler (1 per child)
a heavy book (1 per child)

Questions to ask:
- How do you think a sound is made?
- How do you think sounds get from one place to another?

What to do:
Place a heavy book at the edge of a table or desk. Have each child firmly trap one end of the ruler under the book by holding the book down with his hand. Have him bend down the extended end of the ruler and let it go.

Questions to ask:
- What did you hear?
- What did you see?
- What happened to allow the ruler to make a sound?
- What happened when the ruler stopped moving?

This is why:
Every sound is produced by the vibrations of an object. When an object such as the ruler vibrates, the vibrating object causes the molecules in the air to start vibrating. The vibrations move outward in all directions from the ruler. The vibrations enter your ears, and your brain interprets them as sounds.

Activity 2

You will need:
metal spoons (1 per child)
string (4 feet per child)

What to do:
Pair students for this activity. Have one student in each pair tie a spoon to the middle of a four-foot piece of string. Have him wrap each end of the string around an index finger and place the tip of an index finger in each ear. Have his partner bang the spoon with another spoon. Then have the student pairs switch roles and do the activity again.

Questions to ask:
- What did you hear?
- What did you feel?
- How did the sound get from the spoon to your ears?

Then:
Have the student pairs try this activity again without putting their fingers in their ears.

Questions to ask:
- What did you hear?
- How is this sound different from the first sound?
- Why were the sounds different?

This is why:
Sound waves travel in all directions in air, water, and solids. Sound can move through any material. The metal in the spoon started to vibrate when it was struck. These vibrations were transmitted up the string to the ears. Sound vibrations travel faster through solids than they do through air, which made the sound louder when it traveled up the string. By removing your fingers from your ears, the sound traveled only through the air, making the sound softer.

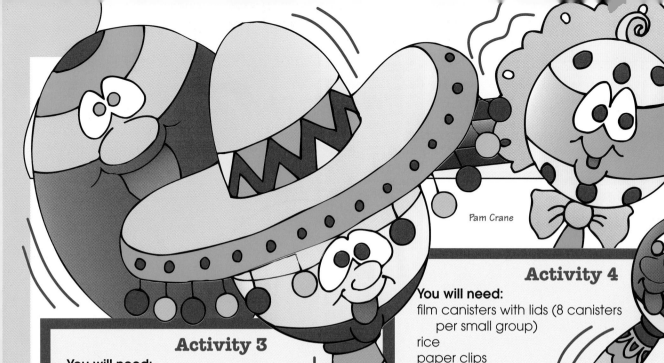

Pam Crane

Activity 3

You will need:
several widemouthed glass jars
(1 for every 2 students)
water
marbles (1 per student)

Questions to ask:
- Do you think you can hear sounds underwater?
- Do you think underwater sounds are loud or soft?
- Do you think sounds are heard more clearly through air or underwater?

What to do:
Fill the jars 2/3 full of water. Place each of the jars on a different table. Place two marbles at each table. Pair the students around each table. Have one of the students bang the marbles under the water while the other student places his ear firmly next to the glass jar. Then have the student pairs switch roles and do the activity again.

Questions to ask:
- Did you hear the sound of the marbles under the water?
- How clear was the sound?
- Was it a loud or a soft sound?

Then:
Have the student pairs try this activity again without putting their ears to the jars.

Questions to ask:
- What did you hear?
- Why was this sound different from the first sound?

This is why:
Sound travels faster through liquids than through air. Since sound travels four times faster through water than through air, you heard the sounds more loudly with your ear pressed against the jar.

Activity 4

You will need:
film canisters with lids (8 canisters
per small group)
rice
paper clips
buttons
pennies

Questions to ask:
- Do all things make the same sound?
- How can you tell the differences between sounds?

What to do:
Partially fill two canisters with rice, two with paper clips, two with buttons, and two with pennies. Place the eight canisters on a table. Color-code the bottom of each canister for self-checking if desired. Have a small group of students take turns shaking the canisters and matching the pairs of canisters that sound alike.

Questions to ask:
- How were the sounds similar?
- How did the sounds differ?
- How were you able to match the two corresponding sounds?

This is how:
The number of sound waves per second produced by a sounding body determines its pitch—the grade of highness or lowness of the sound as perceived by the recipient. The objects in the canisters have their own pitches when shaken. By shaking the canisters and listening carefully, the students could determine which canisters produced the same pitch.

For added fun:
Have each of your youngsters bring in an object from home. Ask students to explore various ways to make several different sounds and pitches with the objects.

"Sound-sational" Books:
Sounds My Feet Make by Arlene Blanchard
Georgia Music by Helen V. Griffith
Ty's One-Man Band by Mildred Pitts Walter
Through Grandpa's Eyes by Patricia MacLachlan

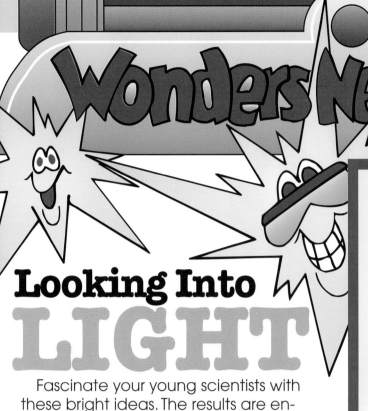

Wonders Never Cease

Looking Into LIGHT

Fascinate your young scientists with these bright ideas. The results are en-lightening!

Activity 1

You will need:
a darkened room
a sunny day

What to do:
On a sunny day, take youngsters outside and ask them to look around and think about what they see. Then go inside and block as much light from your room as you can. Have youngsters look around the room and think about the things that they can see. (If possible, have youngsters look around outside at the end of one school day; then ask youngsters to have their parents take them outside for a few minutes after dark. Have them look around at night to see what they can see.)

Questions to ask:
- What could you see when you were outside during the day?
- What could you see in the dark?
- Why couldn't you see as many things in the dark?

This is why:
We need light to see things. When light shines on an object, some of the light bounces off the object and into our eyes. We can only see things that light falls upon. If light does not shine on something, people cannot see it. (Note to the teacher: We can also see objects that are hot enough to make their own light.)

Activity 2

You will need:
a darkened room
several flashlights
several medium to large bowls of water
several rulers

What to do:
In a darkened room, give each child an opportunity to use a flashlight. Encourage youngsters to turn the flashlights off and on, and point them in several different directions.

Questions to ask:
- Where does the light go when you point the flashlight up? Down? Out to your side?
- Why does the light go in the direction in which you are holding the flashlight?

This is why:
Light travels in straight lines. A straight path of light is called a ray.

Then:
Have each small group of children gather around a different bowl of water and a ruler. Ask children to look at the rulers. Then have one child in each group place the ruler in the water and lean it up against the side of the bowl. After observing the partially submerged ruler, encourage each child to watch the appearance of the ruler as he moves it in and out of the water.

Questions to ask:
- How does the ruler look when it is out of the water?
- How does the ruler look when it is in the water?
- Why does the ruler look bent when it is in the water?

This is why:
Rays of light go through water. The water bends the rays of light. The ruler looks bent because the light rays that are bouncing off it are bent by the water.

Pam Crane

Activity 4

You will need:
6" cardboard circles
short pencils
crayons: red, blue, orange, yellow, green, purple

What to do:
   Draw a straight line dividing a cardboard circle into equal halves. Color one side of the circle red and the other side blue. Poke the pencil through the center of the circle. (If the pencil does not fit snugly in the hole, secure it with a piece of clay.) Have youngsters look at the circle. Then twirl the pencil as if it were a spinning top, and let it go on a smooth, flat surface.

Questions to ask:
• How many colors were on the circle?
• What colors were they?
• How many colors did you see when the circle was spinning?
• What color was it?
• Why did the colors change?

This is why:
   When the circle was spinning, the light rays from both of the colors appeared to be mixed together. Red and blue together make purple, so you saw purple. (Note to the teacher: If you color the sections of a six-sectioned circle in order (red, orange, yellow, green, blue, and purple), the spinning circle will appear white.)

Free exploration:
   For each child provide a six-inch cardboard circle and a short pencil. Have each child (following the procedure above) experiment by making his own spinning color wheel with the colors of his choice.

Activity 3

You will need:
glass prisms
sunny windows
white construction paper

What to do:
   Give each child an opportunity to hold and manipulate a glass prism over a sheet of white construction paper while standing next to a sunny window. Encourage youngsters to move the prisms around until they "catch the light" in their prisms.

Questions to ask:
• What color is the light that passes through the window?
• What happens when the light goes through a prism?
• How many different colors can you see?
• Why did the colors appear?

This is why:
   Most light appears to be white or colorless. But if light shines through a special glass prism, the light bends into its different colors. The colors are called the spectrum. *A rainbow is a spectrum.*

Stargazing

Explore the wonder of stars with this collection of twinkling hands-on activities.

Activity 1

You will need:
a flashlight
a well-lit room
a dark room

What to do:
Seat youngsters along one side of a well-lit room. Stand on the opposite side of the room and shine a flashlight toward them. Repeat the activity with the room darkened or in another dark room.

Questions to ask:
• Is it easier to see the flashlight beam in the light or in the dark?
• Do stars go away during the day?
• Why can't we see stars during the day?

This is why:

The flashlight beam is easier to see in the dark. Stars are always shining, even during the daytime. We can't see stars during the daytime because sunlight brightens the sky. At night, when the sky is dark and clear, stars can be seen.

Activity 2

You will need:
two standard-size flashlights
a large, dark room

What to do:
Have each of two youngsters hold one of the flashlights and stand side by side across the end of a large room. Seat remaining youngsters along the opposite wall; then darken the room. Have the youngsters shine their flashlights toward their classmates.

Stop and ask:
• Which beam of light looks brighter?

Then:
Have one youngster slowly move forward two-thirds of the distance of the room. Have seated youngsters note changes in the brightness of the flashlight beams.

Questions to ask:
• How did the beam of light change as it got closer to us?
• Most stars are very big, but they look very small from earth. Why do you think this is so?

This is why:

The brightness of the two standard-size flashlights probably looked about the same when they were lined up along the wall. As the moving flashlight got closer, it appeared to be brighter and bigger. Objects that are farther away seem smaller. Most stars are about the same size as the sun. They look small from the earth because they are millions of miles away.

71

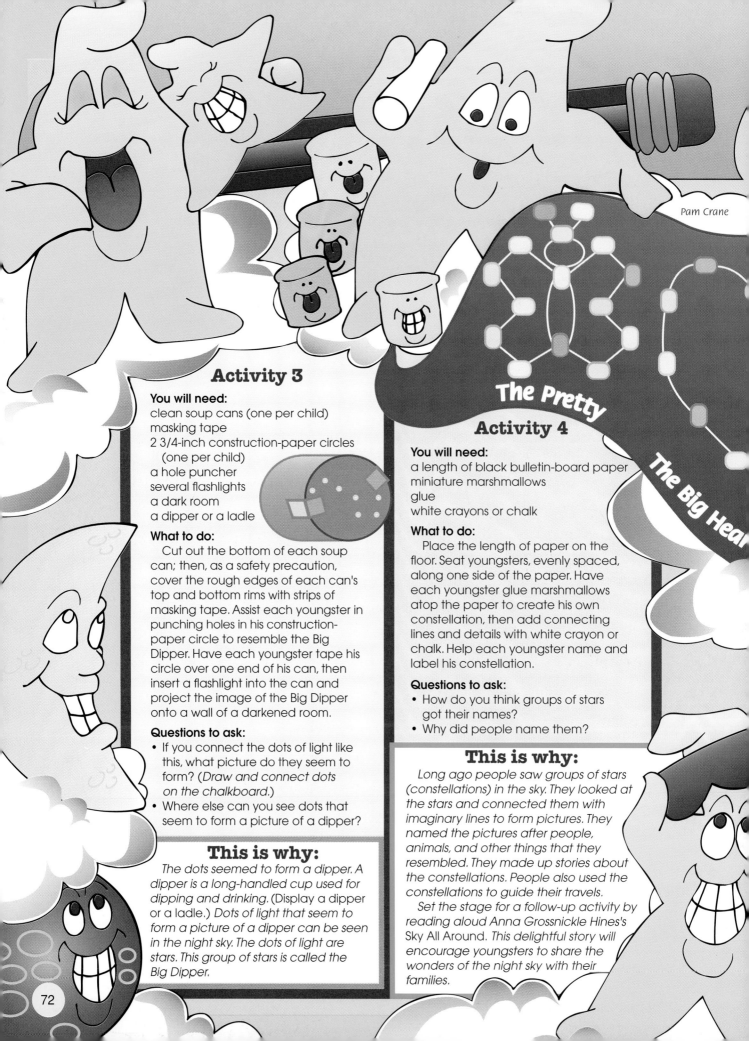

Pam Crane

Activity 3

You will need:
clean soup cans (one per child)
masking tape
2 3/4-inch construction-paper circles
    (one per child)
a hole puncher
several flashlights
a dark room
a dipper or a ladle

What to do:
Cut out the bottom of each soup can; then, as a safety precaution, cover the rough edges of each can's top and bottom rims with strips of masking tape. Assist each youngster in punching holes in his construction-paper circle to resemble the Big Dipper. Have each youngster tape his circle over one end of his can, then insert a flashlight into the can and project the image of the Big Dipper onto a wall of a darkened room.

Questions to ask:
- If you connect the dots of light like this, what picture do they seem to form? (*Draw and connect dots on the chalkboard.*)
- Where else can you see dots that seem to form a picture of a dipper?

This is why:
The dots seemed to form a dipper. A dipper is a long-handled cup used for dipping and drinking. (Display a dipper or a ladle.) *Dots of light that seem to form a picture of a dipper can be seen in the night sky. The dots of light are stars. This group of stars is called the Big Dipper.*

The Pretty
The Big Hear

Activity 4

You will need:
a length of black bulletin-board paper
miniature marshmallows
glue
white crayons or chalk

What to do:
Place the length of paper on the floor. Seat youngsters, evenly spaced, along one side of the paper. Have each youngster glue marshmallows atop the paper to create his own constellation, then add connecting lines and details with white crayon or chalk. Help each youngster name and label his constellation.

Questions to ask:
- How do you think groups of stars got their names?
- Why did people name them?

This is why:
Long ago people saw groups of stars (constellations) in the sky. They looked at the stars and connected them with imaginary lines to form pictures. They named the pictures after people, animals, and other things that they resembled. They made up stories about the constellations. People also used the constellations to guide their travels.

Set the stage for a follow-up activity by reading aloud Anna Grossnickle Hines's Sky All Around. *This delightful story will encourage youngsters to share the wonders of the night sky with their families.*

Incredible Eggs

Crack an egg or an egg book. Either way, incredible learning opportunities await your youngsters!

by Lucia Kemp Henry

Pam Crane

Eggs Change

The incredible egg is a great medium for demonstrating that a liquid can be changed into a solid. First crack a raw egg into a clear, glass bowl. As youngsters describe the appearance of the yolk and white, write the descriptive words on a poster-board egg cutout. Guide the discussion, if necessary, to be certain that the word list includes *liquid*. Ask youngsters how this liquid could be changed into a *solid*. What different ways do they know of to do this?

Hard-boil an egg. (Hard-boil several if you will be making pinwheel sandwiches as described below.) After it has cooled, have students crack open the egg and describe what it looks like, making a list of the descriptive words on a poster-board egg cutout. Guide the discussion, if necessary, to be certain that the word list includes *solid*. Then ask youngsters to describe how the raw egg was different from the cooked egg, using the two word lists for reference.

Pinwheel Sandwiches

Here's a cooking experience your little egg lovers will enjoy. Using your favorite recipe, have students make egg salad. Then have them trim the crusts from slices of wheat bread and spread the egg salad thinly over the bread. Show them how to roll up the bread and slice it crosswise to create 1/2"-thick slices. As your youngsters enjoy their sandwiches, read them an egg book such as *The Egg Book* (Kent), *Green Eggs And Ham* (Seuss), or *Chickens Aren't The Only Ones* (Heller). Or share excerpts from *What's Hatching Out Of That Egg?* (Lauber) or *The Amazing Egg Book* (Griffin and Seed).

I Do Not Like Them!

The cumulative text and catchy rhymes in *Green Eggs And Ham* by Dr. Seuss will have your youngsters egging you on to a tasteful finish. Although the reluctant character in the book did not appear to like green eggs, he may have been happy to try eggs cooked another way. Have your students brainstorm a list of ways to serve eggs as you record their responses on the board. Ask each youngster to choose his favorite style of eggs and graph the results. Conclude the activity by having students prepare and eat scrambled eggs which have been tinted green with food coloring.

73

Guessing Game

Intrigue little egg experts with this guessing activity. Photocopy the egg pocket on page 79 onto white paper. Laminate the pocket and the cards on pages 149 and 151. To make the pocket, cut on the solid lines, fold on the dotted lines, and staple or glue the sides of the egg. Cut apart the animal cards and store them in the egg pocket.

To play, read the conversation balloon that is showing from the top of the egg. Have youngsters take turns guessing the identity of the hatchling. Pull the card from the egg to reveal the correct answer. Continue in this manner until all of the riddles have been answered.

Not From Chickens Only

Share a colorful rhyming book with your youngsters and teach a simple lesson about egg-laying creatures. Ruth Heller's book, *Chickens Aren't The Only Ones*, introduces youngsters to a parade of birds, amphibians, reptiles, fish, and insects—all of whom lay eggs.

Have your youngsters closely examine each egg-layer featured in the book and describe such features as colors, coverings (skin, scales, feathers, etc.), and numbers of legs. Then have students search through back issues of wildlife magazines, clipping pictures of the egg-layers they see. Title a bulletin board "Chickens Aren't The Only Ones That Lay Eggs!" Visually divide the board into five sections and label each section with one of these headings: *birds, amphibians, reptiles, fish,* or *insects.* Assist youngsters as they staple the magazine pictures to the corresponding board sections.

I live in Africa. I hatched from the biggest kind of egg. It weighed about three pounds. When I came out of the egg, I was about a foot tall.

What Am I?

I live near a pond. I hatched from egg that had a gooey covering. M and a thousand others floated together in the pond. The eggs were covered in the jelly. The jelly helpe keep us warm.

frog

Who's In The Egg?

Hatch a lot of fun with this "egg-stra" special action rhyme. Chickens, lizards, turtles, ducks, snakes, fish, octopi, sea horses, frogs, spiders, and ants are just a few of the animals that hatch from eggs. Have your youngsters brainstorm a list of animals that hatch from eggs. Draw simple sketches on the board for several of the animals mentioned. While saying the rhyme, have students make the motions indicated and complete the fourth line with the name of an animal. In doing so, they can imitate the hatching of a different creature each time the verse is repeated.

Pam Crane

Who will it be (*Speak slowly and with a deliberate beat as you cover your face with your arms.*)
Inside the egg?
Can't wait to see!

Tip, tap, crick, crack.
Out pops a [animal name]. (*Fling your arms open wide.*)
And that is that!

Eggshell Planters

Recycle eggshells for use as seed-sprouting containers, and introduce your little ones to the joys of gardening. Collect large, broken eggshell pieces for this activity. Carefully poke a small hole in the bottom of each for water drainage. Write each student's name on a shell. Set them in egg cartons and fill them with potting soil. Have each youngster plant two or three marigold seeds in his shell according to package directions. Set the eggshell planters in a sunny spot and keep them moist by misting with a spray bottle until seeds sprout. Thin the seedlings, leaving one strong seedling in each eggshell container. Water seedlings with care and transplant to a sunny location when they have outgrown the eggshells.

After this experience, give your youngsters opportunities to dictate stories titled "The Flower That Hatched From An Egg!" Then have each youngster draw a large picture of his flower on blue construction paper. Have him use markers to color all but the flower's bloom. Have him trace the lines of his bloom with glue and sprinkle the glue with yellow-tinted, crushed eggshells. Display each youngster's illustration with his story.

Better By The Dozen

This "egg-ceptional" idea may be just the new spring center you're looking for! Reproduce the egg-carton pattern on page 76 onto yellow construction paper. Cut out the carton on the bold line and fold on the fine line. Under the words "Farm Fresh," write a title for your matching game. Color the chicken, eggs, and nest, if desired. Make a dozen eggs using the patterns on page 77. Glue six eggs inside the carton in a row below the fold line. Program these eggs for a matching skill. Beneath each programmed egg, trace the outline of an egg cutout. Program the remaining six eggs to match the ones attached to the carton. Laminate the pieces, if desired. Store the carton and the eggs in a large Ziploc® bag. To use the center, a student places a matching egg cutout below each egg in the carton.

Humpty Dumpty

Your youngsters will agree that this famous egghead also makes a great subject for an art project. For each project you will need: a 12" x 18" sheet of blue construction paper; a 9" x 12" sheet of white construction paper; small, rectangular sponge pieces; red tempera paint; glue; scissors; crayons; and a white construction-paper copy of the pieces on page 78. To begin, draw and color a face near the top of the egg shape. Color Humpty's hat, arms, and legs; then cut out the pieces. Glue the white paper on the lower half of the construction paper. Sponge-print red tempera paint onto the white paper to represent a red brick wall. Arrange the pieces for the desired Humpty Dumpty pose, and glue him in place. If desired, display these art projects on a bulletin board surrounding a copy of the nursery rhyme.

Pam Crane

Good Eggs

For all their hard work, your youngsters deserve recognition. Duplicate the award on page 77 for each of them. Then, when a student makes an "egg-ceptional" effort, present him with a completed copy of the award.

Pattern

Use with "Better By The Dozen" on page 75. Reproduce this pattern on yellow construction paper.

Farm Fresh

Reproduce eggs on white construction paper.

Reproduce 12 eggs for each matching game.

Hoorah!

_____
(student)

is really a GOOD EGG!

_____
(teacher)

©1997 The Education Center, Inc. • *THE BEST OF* THE MAILBOX® *SCIENCE* • Pre/K • TEC1458

77

Patterns
Use with "Humpty Dumpty" on page 75.

What Am I?

Science For Early Childhood Teachers

Just Ducky

Get "quackin' " with this fine-feathered collection of duck-related science activities. You'll create a splash of hands-on fun!
ideas contributed by Margie Dunlevy

Activity 1

You will need:
cloth feather cutouts (two per child)
solid vegetable shortening
    (such as Crisco®)
a bowl
water
several droppers

What to do:
   Fill a bowl with water. Place the droppers near the bowl. Have each youngster coat both sides of a feather cutout with vegetable shortening. Next have each young- ster drop several drops of water onto an uncoated feather cutout. Then have him repeat the procedure using his coated cutout.

Questions to ask:
- What happened when you dropped water onto the uncoated feather?
- What happened when you dropped water onto the coated feather?
- Why did the water bead up on the coated feather?
- How do you think a duck water- proofs its feathers?

This is why:
Water soaked into the uncoated feather. But water beaded up on the coated feather because it was covered with waxy shortening. Ducks waterproof their feathers with a waxy oil. The oil is produced in a gland at the base of the duck's tail. The duck uses its bill to rub its feathers with the oil.

Activity 2

You will need:
a large pot
water
a long-handled spoon
birdseed
weeds
grass
a strainer
paper towels

What to do:
   Fill the pot half full of water. Have youngsters stir in small handfuls of birdseed and small bits of weeds and grass. Then, in turn, have each youngster dip the strainer into the pot, lift the strainer out of the water, and let the water drain back into the pot. Then have each youngster empty the con- tents of the strainer onto a paper towel.

Questions to ask:
- What happened when you lifted the strainer out of the water?
- Why do you think some ducks have broad bills that let the water out?

This is why:
When the strainer was lifted from the water, it separated the birdseed, weeds, and grass from the water. The water drained back into the pot. Some ducks' bills act like strainers, too. Some ducks dabble. They take in a mouthful of water containing seeds, weeds, grass, and insects, then let the water drain out of the sides of their toothlike bills. In this way, dabbling ducks are able to separate their food from the water where it is found.

Activity 3

You will need:
a large tub
water
gallon-size plastic bags
   (one per child)
rubber bands

What to do:
   Fill the large tub half full of water. Have each child roll up his sleeves and place a plastic bag over one of his hands. Secure each child's bag in place around his wrist with a loosely fitting rubber band. Have the child spread apart the fingers on both of his hands. Then have him place both hands in the water and move his hands in a paddling motion resembling that of a duck.

Questions to ask:
- Which of your hands was harder to pull through the water? Why?
- Which of your hands made a better "paddle"? Why?
- Why do you think ducks are such good swimmers?

This is why:
   The hand covered by the plastic bag was harder to pull through the water. Water passes easily between the fingers of the uncovered hand, but it cannot pass between the fingers covered by the plastic bag, so the hand covered by the plastic bag also made a better paddle. Ducks have webbed feet that act as paddles and help them swim well.

Activity 4

You will need:
a large open area
several pairs of flippers

What to do:
   Have each student don a pair of flippers, then squat and walk like a duck.

Questions to ask:
- Why was it hard for you to squat and walk while wearing flippers?
- Why is it hard for a duck to walk on land?

This is why:
   Short legs and wide, flat feet make it hard to walk. Ducks have short legs and webbed feet that are made for swimming, so ducks waddle clumsily when they walk on land.

Pam Crane

Window On Weather

Gather together for a unit filled with weather facts and fun.

by Lucia Kemp Henry

Springtime Is Stormy

Springtime means stormy weather in many regions of the United States. This changeable weather can bring rain, wind, thunderstorms, tornadoes, and sometimes even snow! During a circle time, discuss the kinds of stormy spring weather that are common in your region of the country. Brainstorm a list of words that describe your local springtime weather. Title the list "Springtime Weather." Have each youngster tell about experiences he has had in any type of springtime weather.

After your discussion, narrow your youngsters' focus to the topic of *stormy* weather. Encourage them to think about the things in the environment that warn that a storm is coming. Students can again list their ideas in a brainstorming session. You might wish to divide the list into two categories. One group can list warnings found in nature, while the other group lists warnings that are man-made. This discussion is also a convenient springboard for introducing or reviewing storm safety practices.

Stormy Weather

Warnings in nature	Man-made warnings
_____	_____
_____	_____
_____	_____
_____	_____

Weather Watcher's Chart

Reinforce your little ones' weather observation skills with this take-home weather-watching project. For each child, duplicate the "Weather Watcher's Report" (page 85) onto brightly colored copy paper. Also duplicate the weather wheel pattern (page 84) and the weather report pages (page 86) onto construction paper. Have each child write his name on the weather watcher's report; then glue it to a piece of tagboard or cereal-box cardboard. Have adults use X-acto® knives to cut out the sections indicated by dotted lines. Then cut out the weather wheel and use a brad to attach one wheel to the back of each child's chart. Have each child add illustrations to his weather report pages; then cut along the dotted lines. Stack the pages and staple them to the weather watcher's report where indicated. (Use a small stapler and slip it through the cut-out area or use a stapler with a long reach.)

Ask each child to take his weather watcher's report home so he can report the weather to his family. Each day he can observe the weather and turn the wheel to show the weather word for the day. Then he can show the matching illustration by sliding the unrelated pages on top through the cut-out area above the pictures.

I see **sunshine**.

I see **clouds**.

Weather Watcher's Report by **Kenny**

The weather today is: **rainy**

I see **rain**.

Watching The Weather

A major component of any scientific study is observation. Give your students the opportunity to observe and record scientific data with this activity. Make a large calendar for the month of April on poster board. Be sure that the squares on the calendar are at least 3" x 3" to fit the calendar pictures on page 84. Duplicate the patterns (page 84) several times onto construction paper; then color and cut them out. Each morning, have your children observe and discuss the weather. Select a calendar picture to represent that day's weather and post it on the calendar. If the weather changes during the course of the day, be sure to have children reevaluate and possibly add to their weather observations!

At the end of the month, have your students look at the completed weather calendar and tell you some facts about the weather that month. Ask which type of weather was the most frequent/least frequent. If desired, have children substantiate their observations by cutting apart the calendar squares and arranging them in graph form.

April

Sunday	Monday	Tuesday	Wednesday	Thursday	Friday	Saturday
						sunny
sunny	sunny	cloudy	cloudy	rainy	rainy	8
9	10	11	12	13	14	15
16	17	18	19	20	21	22
23 / 30	24	25	26	27	28	29

Spring Weather Song

Enlarge and duplicate the calendar pictures (page 84) onto construction paper. Have children color and cut out the patterns; then glue them to wooden craft sticks. As you sing the song below, have children hold up the appropriate pictures.

(adapted to the tune of "Jack And Jill")
Springtime weather, it can change.
Oh, it can change each da-ay.
In the spring we might see **clouds**.
I love a **cloudy** da-ay!

Repeat the song, replacing the boldfaced word pair with each of these word pairs in turn: *rain/rainy, snow/snowy, wind/windy,* and *sun/sunny.*

What's Your Pleasure?

This activity will reinforce graphing skills as well as provide a means for children to make predictions, draw conclusions, and express their opinions. For each child, duplicate the weather pictures (page 88) onto construction paper. Direct each child to cut the pictures apart on the bold lines. Ask each child to color the pictures; then have her secretly select one picture to represent her favorite type of weather. (Collect the extra pictures and save them to play Weather Charades.) Have each child hold her weather picture so that it cannot be seen. Then ask students to predict which type of weather they think will be most- and least-liked. Label a sheet of chart paper with the four weather headings, and have each child tape her selected weather picture under the appropriate one. Discuss what the graph reveals and how the actual outcome compares to the predictions.

Window-On-Weather Booklet

Use a variety of art projects to create a "peek-through" booklet highlighting springtime weather. For each child, duplicate the weather booklet page (page 87) four times on construction paper. Cut out the window spaces on all of the pages. Then, for each child, cut four plain white pages to match the 7 1/4" x 9" booklet pages. Write a different weather sentence on the bottom of each of the four plain pages: "The weather is cloudy," "The weather is windy," "The weather is rainy," and "The weather is sunny." Then prepare four different art stations (described below) to complete each page in a different style. When each page is complete, place a cut-out window page over each art page. Staple all of the pages together and personalize the top page.

Cloudy Art: Draw and color clouds with a crayon. (Apply the crayon heavily.) Dab very diluted black or blue tempera paint over the clouds with cotton balls. The crayon will resist the paint and create an interesting effect.

Windy Art: Drop a small amount of watery paint on the lower portion of the paper. Use a straw to blow the paint towards the upper portion of the paper. Glue on small construction-paper leaves.

Rainy Art: Cut pieces of foam meat trays into sections. Use a ballpoint pen to press deep, rainlike lines into the foam. To make a handle, glue a square of old sponge or a wooden spool to the back of each foam piece. Press a foam piece into slightly thinned tempera paint; then print the "rain" on the page. Repeat the process for the desired effect.

Sunny Art: Cut out a sun shape from construction paper. Use a wide brush to brush water-diluted glue on the sun. Then cover the sun with tissue-paper scraps. Using vibrant, sunny colors of tempera paint, paint over the tissue paper. When the paint is dry, trim the excess tissue paper if necessary; then glue the sun to the book page.

Weather Charades

Use the leftover cards from "What's Your Pleasure?" for charade cards. Place the cards facedown in a basket or box lid. To play, have one child choose a card, look at the card, and place it facedown in a discard pile. Then encourage that child to act out the type of weather that was pictured on his card. He may choose to portray how a person would react in that particular type of weather or he may even pretend to *be* the weather. Give each child an opportunity to choose a card and playact. Just remember—not a word may be spoken!

Barry Slate

83

Patterns
calendar pictures

Use with "Watching The Weather" on page 82 and "Spring Weather Song" on page 83.

weather wheel

Use with "Weather Watcher's Chart" on page 82.

snowy

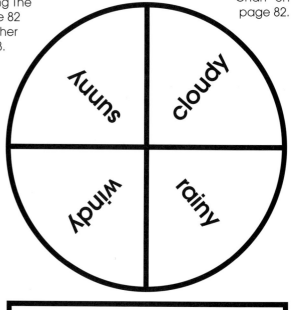

cloudy

rainy

windy

sunny

Weather Watcher's Report

by

The weather today is:

Cut out.

Cut out.

Staple weather picture pages here.

I see **rain**.

I see **clouds**.

I see **wind**.

I see **sunshine**.

Pattern
weather booklet page
Use with "Window-On-Weather Booklet" on page 83.

What is the weather?

©1997 The Education Center, Inc.

©1997 The Education Center, Inc.

©1997 The Education Center, Inc.

©1997 The Education Center, Inc.

Wonders Never Cease

It's Raining, It's Pouring

Your students will shower you with interest and excitement when doing these hands-on activities related to dazzling, drizzling, dripping rain!

Pam Crane

Activity 1

You will need:
an ice cube tray
a kettle one-quarter filled with water
a hot plate

What to do:
Heat the kettle of water. When the water is boiling, hold the ice cube tray about five inches down into the vapor coming from the kettle's spout. Ask students to watch and comment on what happens beneath the ice cube tray.

Questions to ask:
- What happened when the warm vapor touched the cold ice cube tray?
- Why do you think the vapor formed drops on the bottom of the tray?
- What happened to each drop after it had been on the tray bottom for a while?
- Why is the water that drips from the bottom of the tray a lot like rain?

This is why:
The ice cube tray suddenly cooled the warm water vapor that came from the kettle spout. When the vapor cooled, it condensed into water drops and fell to the floor. This process is similar to what happens on a rainy day. Cooled condensed drops of water vapor fall to earth.

Activity 2

You will need:
a rainy day without lightning or thunder
black construction paper for each child
an umbrella

What to do:
Have students take turns standing under an umbrella and holding construction paper in the rain so that a few drops strike it. Caution students not to permit the paper to be soaked. Return inside to observe the papers.

Questions to ask:
- Do the raindrops on your paper look alike?
- How are the raindrops different?
- Are raindrops all the same size and shape? Why or why not?

This is why:
There will be many different sizes of water drops on the construction paper because raindrops are not all the same size. A drop of rain is made up of water molecules clinging together. Small raindrops have fewer molecules of water. As molecules of water stick together, they form bigger drops.

Activity 3

You will need:
a couple of rainy days
a clear plastic container with straight sides
a plastic ruler
a permanent marker

What to do:
Tape the plastic ruler to the side of the jar so that the ruler reads from the bottom to the top. Place the jar in the rain. When the rain stops or at the end of the day, mark the level that the rain reached. Pour out the rain, and repeat the exercise on another rainy day.

Questions to ask:
- Who might want to know how much rain has fallen?
- What happens when there is too much (too little) rain?
- What do you call something that measures rain?
- Did we catch the same amount of rain on both rainy days? Why or why not?

This is why:
Rainfall can vary greatly. The amount of rainfall affects humans, plants, and animals. Meteorologists, scientists who study weather, measure rainfall using instruments called rain gauges.

Wonders Never Cease

Sunny Days

What warms the earth and the objects in and on it? Why do some objects hold more heat than others? Try these sunny-day activities with your youngsters and find out!

Activity 1

For each small group, you will need:
a resealable plastic bag
chocolate chips

What to do:
For each small group, place their materials on a table. Ask youngsters to put a few of the chips in the plastic bag, seal it, and place the bag near a window that allows bright sunshine in. Leave the bags undisturbed, and come back to observe their contents in about 30 minutes.

Questions to ask:
- How did the chips look/feel when you put them in the bag?
- How do the chips look/feel now?
- Why do you think the chips look and feel different?

This is why:
The sun warmed the window, and the heat in the window radiated to the air around it. Since the chips were placed near the window, the heat melted them.

Activity 2

For each small group, you will need:
two rocks

What to do:
Have each small group examine its rocks, paying particular attention to the temperature of each rock. Then direct each group to place one of its rocks in a shady spot on the playground and to place the other in a bright, sunny spot. Leave the rocks undisturbed, and come back to observe them in about one hour.

Questions to ask:
- How did each of the rocks feel before you placed it outside?
- How does the rock that was placed in the sun feel?
- How does the rock that was placed in the shade feel?
- Why do the rocks feel the way they do?

This is why:
The rock that was left in the sun feels warmer because it was heated by the sun's rays. The rock that was left in the shade feels cooler because the sun's rays were blocked by the shade and did not heat the rock.

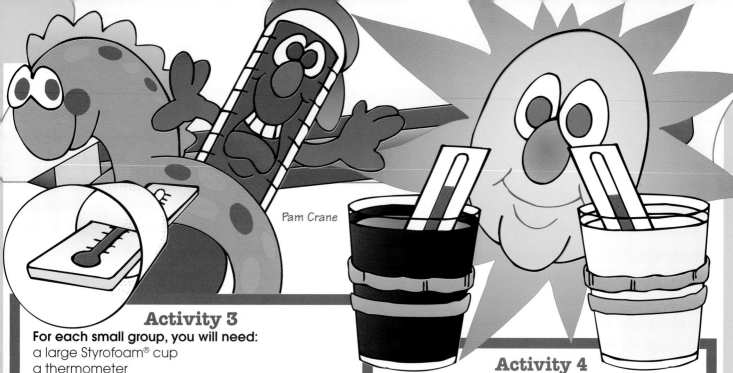

Pam Crane

Activity 3

For each small group, you will need:
a large Styrofoam® cup
a thermometer
a thermometer picture
a red crayon

What to do:

Help each small group push its thermometer partially through the bottom of the cup as shown. (The cup is useful in protecting the thermometer from direct sunlight, which could alter the results.) Assign each group a specific location from which to work such as on a concrete sidewalk, on blacktop, under a piece of playground equipment, or in the shade of a tree. Have each group set its thermometer in its designated area for about five minutes. Then have the group members look at the thermometer to see where the red line stopped. Have one group member find the matching numeral on the thermometer picture and color the center section of the thermometer from that point down. When each group has recorded its results, gather together for a class discussion. (Help students discover that the longer lines represent the hotter temperatures.) Graph the results on the board or on a piece of chart paper.

Questions to ask:
• Which places were the warmest?
• Which places were the coolest?
• Which places were in between in temperature?
• Why is the air warm in some places and cool in other places?

This is why:

The sunny places were warmer because the sun's rays heated them. In the shady places, the sun's rays were blocked or weaker, so those temperatures were cooler.

Activity 4

For each small group, you will need:
two glasses   four thermometer
four rubber bands   pictures
white construction paper   a red crayon
black construction paper   a blue crayon
two thermometers   water

What to do:

For each group, wrap one glass with white construction paper and secure the paper with rubber bands. Similarly wrap the second glass with black construction paper. Fill both glasses with the same amount of water (at the same temperature). Put a thermometer in each glass. Set both glasses in a shaded area of your classroom. After about 30 minutes, check the temperature in each glass and use the blue crayon to color the results on two of the thermometer pictures (the temperatures should be the same). Then place the glasses in a very sunny area for 30 minutes. Again check the temperatures and use a red crayon to color the results on the remaining thermometer pictures.

Questions to ask:
• What were the water temperatures in the shade?
• Were the temperatures the same?
• What were the water temperatures in the sun?
• Were those temperatures the same? Why not?

This is why:

Dark colors absorb more heat than light colors. Therefore, the glass wrapped in black paper was hotter than the glass wrapped in white paper.

Thinking:
• On a very hot summer day, would it be better to wear dark-colored or light-colored clothing? Why?

93

Sinkers Or Floaters?

Why do some objects sink and others float in water? Your youngsters will plunge into these hands-on science activities as they learn about the concepts of sinking and floating.

by Marie Iannetti

Activity 1

You will need:

water
one of each of the following per small group:

large glass bowl	metal paper clip
cork	penny
feather	shoebox
stick	

What to do:

Place one of each of the objects in a shoebox. Place a shoebox on each table. Seat a small group of youngsters around each table. Have each child carefully examine the objects in the shoebox.

Questions to ask: (Record your students' predictions on chart paper or a chalkboard.)

- Which objects do you think will sink in water? Why?
- Which objects do you think will float in water? Why?

What to do:

Fill the bowls 3/4 full of water. Place each of the bowls on a different table. Have each child in a small group take turns dropping the objects into the bowl one at a time. Ask each child to carefully examine what happens to each object after it is dropped in the bowl of water.

Questions to ask:

- Which objects floated in the water?
- Why do you think these objects floated?
- Which objects sank in the water?
- Why do you think they sank?
- How did your predictions recorded earlier differ from what happened?
- How many of your predictions were correct?

This is why:

When an object is placed in water, it pushes some of the water away. This is referred to as water displacement. Objects such as the cork, stick, and feather displace more water than their own weight and therefore they float. Objects such as the stones, paper clips, and pennies sink because there is not enough of an upward push from water to support them.

Activity 2

You will need:

glass bowls (1 per small group)
baby food jars with lids (1 per small group)
water

Questions to ask:

- Do you think a baby food jar will sink or float when placed in a bowl of water? Why?

What to do:

Fill the bowls 3/4 full of water. Place each of the bowls on a table, and assign students to each bowl. Secure the lid on each empty baby food jar. Have one student in each group place the baby food jar in the bowl of water. Ask your students to carefully examine what happens to the jar.

Questions to ask:

- What happened to the jar?
- Why do you think the jar floated?

Then:

Have your youngsters take the jars out of the bowls and remove the lids. Have another student in each group place the jar into the bowl. Have him tip the baby food jar on its side.

Questions to ask:

- What happened to the jar?
- Why do you think the jar sank to the bottom of the bowl?

This is why:

The weight of the empty jar with the lid was less than the weight of the water that it pushed away or displaced. That is why the jar floated. When the lidless baby food jar was tipped on its side, it filled with water. The weight of the water-filled jar was more than the weight of the water it displaced. Therefore the jar sank.

Pam Crane

Activity 3

You will need:
glass tanks or bowls (1 per small group)
modeling clay (1 ball per small group)
water

Questions to ask:
• What do you think will happen when a ball of clay is dropped into a bowl of water?
• Why do you think so?

What to do:
Fill the bowls 3/4 full of water. Place each of the bowls and a ball of modeling clay on a different table. Group students around each table. Have one student in each group place the ball of clay in the water.

Questions to ask:
• What happened to the ball of clay?
• Why did that happen?
• Do you think the shape of the clay made a difference in what happened to it?

What to do:
Have another student in the group retrieve the clay and shape it into a cup-shaped boat. Have him carefully place the boat on the water.

Questions to ask:
• What happened to the boat?
• Why do you think the shape of the clay made a difference?

This is why:
The clay ball sank because it was molded into a small shape. A small amount of water tried to hold up the weight of the ball. There was not enough upward push or water pushed away to support it. The shape of the boat was bigger than the ball of clay, so it pushed more water away. Because it displaced more water, it received a stronger upward push from the water. The push supported the boat so it was able to float.

Activity 4

You will need:
one of each of the following per small group:
    glass
    teaspoon
    raw egg
    plastic self-locking bag partially filled with salt water

Questions to ask:
• Do you think a raw egg will sink or float in water? Why?

What to do:
Give each group a glass and a raw egg. Fill the glasses 3/4 full of water. Have a student from each group place the egg in the water.

Questions to ask:
• What happened to the egg when it was placed in the water?
• Why did this happen?
• What do you think will happen if salt is added to the water?

Then:
Have a student from each group remove the egg from the glass. Give each group a plastic bag 1/2 full of salt. Have a child stir 8 teaspoons of salt into the water before replacing the egg. Ask the youngsters to carefully examine what happens to the egg.
*Important note: Fresh eggs will not float to the top of the water as easily as older ones; therefore more salt may be needed to make the egg float.

Questions to ask:
• What happened when salt was added to the water?
• Why do you think this happened?

This is why:
Because salt water is heavier than freshwater, it pushes harder on objects. Salt water holds up heavier objects than freshwater; therefore objects such as the egg float easier on salt water.

Ladybug And Friends

'Tis the season to crawl into this multi-disciplinary unit on ladybugs and other insects!

by Lucia Kemp Henry

Ladybug Puppet

This lovely ladybug puppet can be used as a special "guest speaker" during your study of insects, or you could have each child make a puppet for his very own. To make a ladybug puppet, use the patterns on page 99. (The patterns given are sized to fit a child's hand.) Cut two body pieces from black felt and two wing pieces from red felt. (The color suggestions given are for a common ladybug. However, since ladybugs come in many different colors, adapt the colors if desired.) Glue or stitch the two body pieces together, leaving the straight edge open. Then glue the red wing pieces to one side of the ladybug. To make the ladybug's spots, glue on black buttons or felt circles. Then, using craft glue or hot glue, attach pipe-cleaner antennae. Well, hello there, little ladybug! How do you do?

I'd Like To Introduce You!

If you made the ladybug puppet (above), have her introduce her insect friends to your class. (Substitute a construction-paper ladybug stick puppet if an alternative is needed.) In advance, cut out the insect pictures on pages 153 and 155 and prepare them for flannelboard use by backing them with felt or sandpaper.

Gather your little ones together. Patterned after the text of *Brown Bear, Brown Bear, What Do You See?* by Bill Martin, Jr., roughly follow the script below.

Children: "Ladybug, Ladybug, what do you see?"

(Place one of the insect characters on the flannelboard.)

Ladybug (Puppeteer): "I see a [butterfly] looking at me."

Children: "[Butterfly, Butterfly], what do you see?"
"I see a [bumblebee] looking at me."
"[Bumblebee, Bumblebee], what do you see?"
"I see a...."

Continue in the same manner until all of the insect characters are displayed on the board. Inserting the name of the last insect to be displayed, continue as follows:

Children: "[Grasshopper, Grasshopper], what do you see?"

(Teacher gestures toward ladybug puppet.)

Children: "I see a ladybug looking at me."
"Ladybug, Ladybug, what do you see?"

Ladybug (Puppeteer): "I see *all* the insects looking at me!"

How Can You Tell?

To some people, bugs are just bugs. But your youngsters will be proud to be able to identify a true insect when they see one. Tell children that all insects have six legs and three main body parts—a head, a thorax, and an abdomen. (All three of a ladybug's body parts can only be seen from its underside.) Then read aloud portions of *Bugs* by Nancy Winslow Parker and Joan Richards Wright. For each bug featured, share the large-print text with your students; then show the large illustration on the following page. Encourage youngsters to determine whether or not that particular bug is an insect by counting its legs and body parts. If your students would be interested to know more facts about each of the featured insects, read the accompanying text ahead of time so that you'll be able to paraphrase the information for your students.

Ladybug, Where Are You?

Making and reading this booklet will give each child a chance to recognize the insects that were shown in "I'd Like To Introduce You!" as well as provide opportunities to practice reading position and sight words. For each child, duplicate the booklet page patterns (pages 100–103) on white construction paper. Equip an art station with small, oval sponge shapes and tempera paints. For each booklet page (except the last), help children read the text; then have them make sponge prints of ladybugs in the appropriate places. Have each child make a print anywhere on the last page. When the prints are dry, youngsters can add spots and antennae with cotton swabs and paint. To complete the last page, have each child cut out a construction-paper leaf that is large enough to cover the ladybug print. Then glue just the end of the leaf onto the page to make a "peek flap" that rests over the ladybug. Have each child illustrate his title page; then cut out all of the pages. Stack all the pages and set them aside.

Provide supplies for each child to make his own booklet cover, or use the patterns on pages 104 and 105. To make a booklet cover using the patterns, duplicate the front booklet cover onto red construction paper and the back booklet cover onto black construction paper. Cut out the patterns. Place the red piece over the stacked booklet pages, aligning the straight, top edges. Then place the red body piece and pages on top of the black body piece, aligning the bottom rounded edges. Staple all the layers together along the top of the red body piece. Glue on pipe-cleaner antennae; then color or paint on spots as desired. When you read the last page, lift the leaf. Yoo-hoo—oh, Ladybug!

by Alex Butner

The Insect Song

Coax the wiggles out of anyone with this song! Use your ladybug puppet and the flannelboard insects (see "Ladybug Puppet" and "I'd Like To Introduce You!" on page 96) to introduce this song to your boys and girls. Then encourage youngsters to develop movements for each insect. As you sing together, give children the run of the room to perform!

(adapted to the tune of "Three Blind Mice")
Buzz, buzz, buzz.
Bumblebees buzz.
Buzz over here.
Buzz over there.
They **buzz** up high and they **buzz** down low.
Around and around and around they go.
They **buzz-buzz** fast, and they **buzz-buzz** slow.
Oh, **bumblebees buzz!**

Repeat the song, replacing the boldfaced insect name and its corresponding action word with each of these word pairs in turn: *grasshoppers/hop, butterflies/flutter, little ants/run, ladybugs/fly, crickets/jump.*

Rhyme Time!

If a reading of *Bugs* (see "How Can You Tell?") has primed your children for a little rhyming practice, try making this insect-related big book. Give each child a large sheet of construction paper. Ask her to think of an insect and a word that rhymes with that insect. Then encourage each child to make up a sentence or two using those two words and illustrate it. If needed, give examples such as "A bug in a jug"; "There are ants on my pants!"; and "A fly on the pie? Oh, my!" Then bind all of the pages between construction-paper covers and title the book as a class. Have each child share her page during a group reading time.

Ladybug And Friends: Poem And Play

The following poem can be practiced and recited or developed into a play. To make costumes for a play, cut arm and head openings in large paper bags. Paint or color the bags to represent the insects in the poem. Put the finishing touches on each costume by making a construction-paper headband with stapled-on pipe-cleaner antennae.

Little red ladybug sits on a leaf.
She sits on a leaf on a tree.
And as she sits on that little green leaf,
There are so many friends to see!

Little yellow bumblebees buzz by the leaf.
They buzz by the leaf on the tree.
And as they buzz by that little green leaf,
There are so many friends to see!

Continue saying the poem, substituting the insect and its action with the suggestions below. Then end the poem with the last stanza.

—Little brown crickets go chirping by the leaf...
—Little tiny ants go scurrying by the leaf...
—Little green grasshoppers go hopping by the leaf...
—Little shy butterflies go fluttering by the leaf...

All the little insects sitting by the leaf.
They sit by the leaf on the tree.
And as they sit by that little green leaf,
They're a happy insect family!

Buggy Bulletin Board

Your classroom will be buzzing with activity when you set up the following art stations and encourage youngsters to create their own insects. Mount the finished projects on a bulletin board.

Station One: Ladybug
Use the ladybug booklet cover patterns on pages 104 and 105 to make tracers from tagboard. Provide different colors of construction paper, buttons, fabric scraps, shiny wrapping paper, scissors, and glue. Display a selection of ladybug pictures and encourage students to create realistic or fantastic ladybugs.

Station Two: Butterfly
Stock this center with different colors of tempera paint or acrylic craft paint, thin paper plates, construction paper, scissors, and glue. To make a butterfly, fold a paper plate in half; then open it up. Dab small dots and lines of various colors of paint on one side of the plate. Refold the plate in half and press the halves together lightly; then unfold the plate. When the paint is dry, refold the plate and cut out half a butterfly shape on the fold. If desired add a construction-paper body and antennae.

Station Three: Fancy Wings
The actual subject of this art station is each artist's choice! A child could make a bee, a dragonfly, a moth—any insect with wings. Provide several different colors of crayon shavings, construction paper, waxed paper, crayons, scissors, and glue. To make an insect, cut out and glue together a construction-paper insect body and add crayon details as desired. Then sprinkle a small amount of crayon shavings between two pieces of waxed paper. Have an adult volunteer place a double thickness of newspaper over the waxed paper and press it with a warm iron. When it has cooled, cut wing shapes from the waxed paper and glue them to the thorax of the insect.

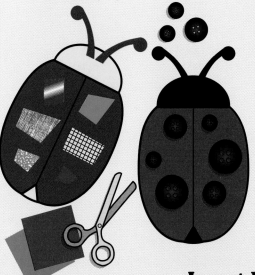

Insect Math

With all these insects running around, math opportunities seem to be crawling out of the woodwork! Photocopy a supply of the insect patterns on page 103. Color them; then cut them apart and use them for the following activities.

Patterning
Place a supply of cut-out insects in a box lid; then place them in a center with sentence strips and glue. Encourage students to make patterns by gluing their insects onto sentence strips. Youngsters might create patterns of their own or continue modeled patterns.

Insect Number Book
Give each child one sheet of construction paper for a title page, and one additional sheet for each number that he'd like to include in his book. (For example, if one child would like to include the numbers 10–20 in his book, give him 12 sheets of paper.) To make one page, have a child write a numeral and the corresponding number word on a sheet of paper. Then have him glue that many of the same insect on the page. Repeat the process for each page. Ambitious students might even like to write and illustrate an original rhyming text to go with each page.

How Much Is 100?
Well—let's see! Cut ten equally sized strips of construction paper long enough to hold ten insect cutouts each. Give each small group of children a construction-paper strip and ask them to glue ten insects to the strip. Then glue each of the strips to a sheet of chart paper. You see? That's 100!

Literature Links

Nonfiction

Big Bugs
Written by Jerry Booth
Illustrated by Edith Allgood
Published by Harcourt Brace & Company

The Ladybug And Other Insects
Created by Gallimard Jeunesse and Pascale de Bourgoing
Illustrated by Sylvie Perols
Published by Scholastic Inc.

Monarchs
Written by Kathryn Lasky
Photographed by Christopher G. Knight
Published by Harcourt Brace & Company

Weird And Wonderful Insects
Written by Sue Hadden
Published by Thomas Learning

Fiction

Billy's Beetle
Written & Illustrated by Mick Inkpen
Published by Harcourt Brace Jovanovich

Fireflies!
Written & Illustrated by Julie Brinckloe
Published by Macmillan Publishing Company

I Wish I Were A Butterfly
Written by James Howe
Illustrated by Ed Young
Published by Harcourt Brace & Company

Ladybug On The Move
Written & Illustrated by Richard Fowler
Published by Harcourt Brace Jovanovich

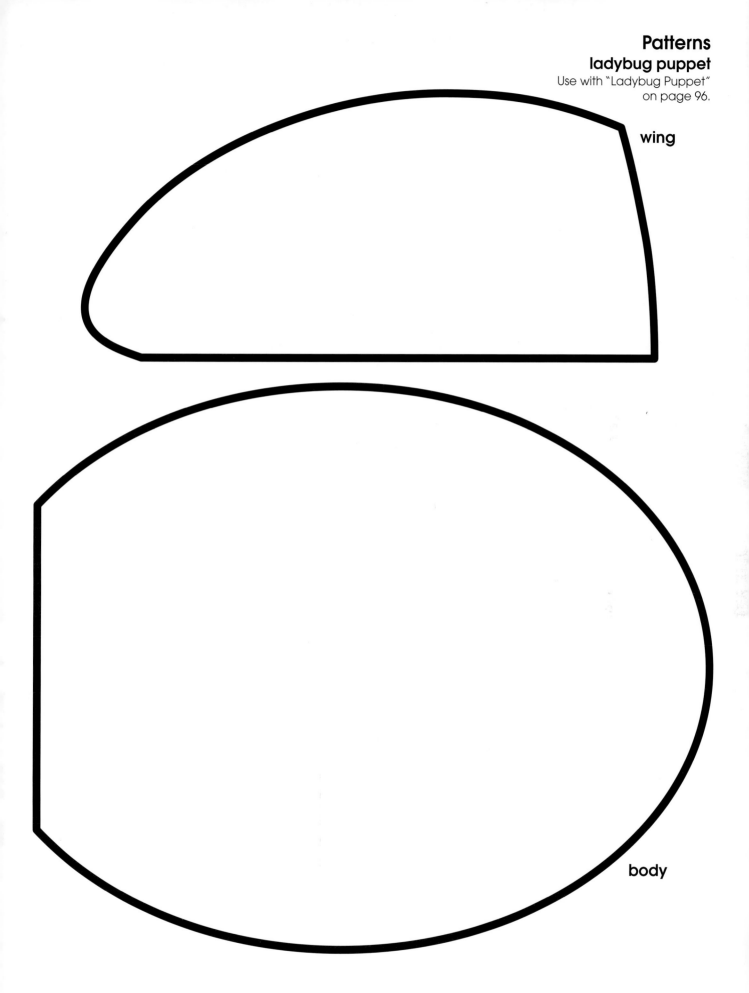

wing

body

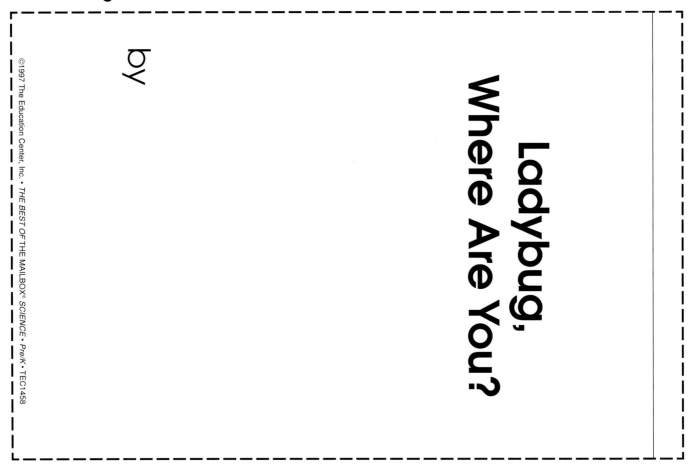

Ladybug, Where Are You?

by

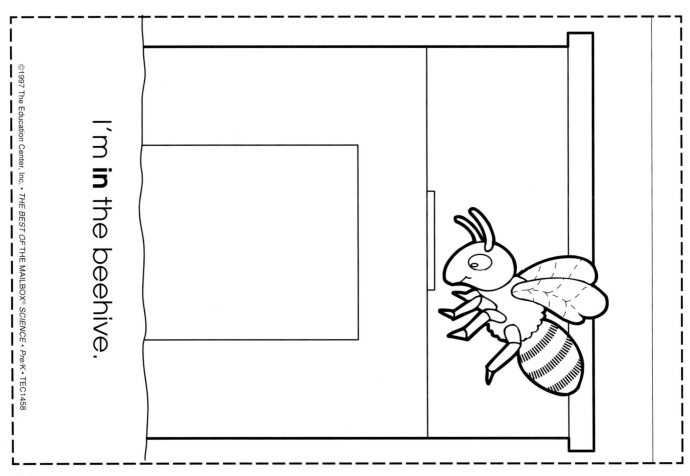

I'm **in** the beehive.

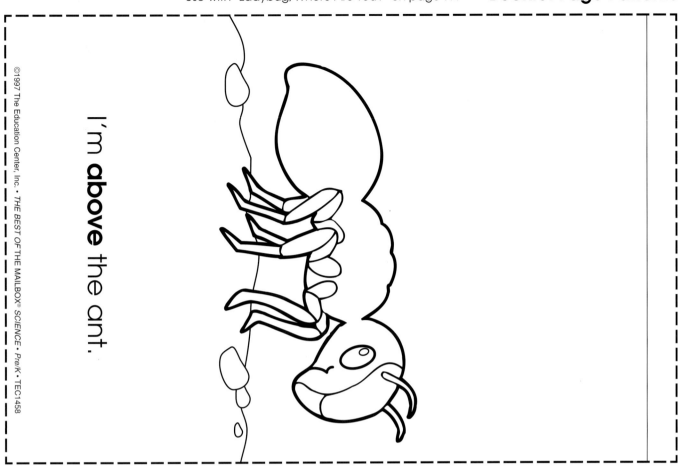

I'm **above** the ant.

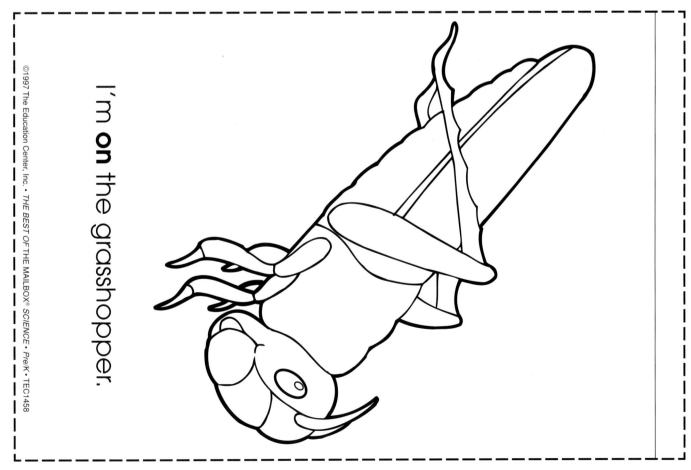

I'm **on** the grasshopper.

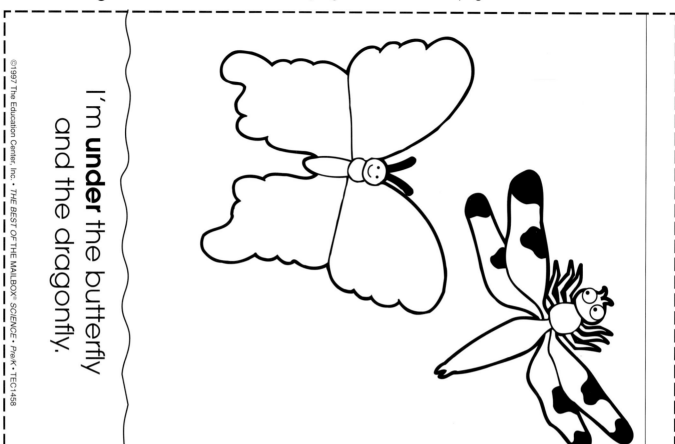

I'm **under** the butterfly and the dragonfly.

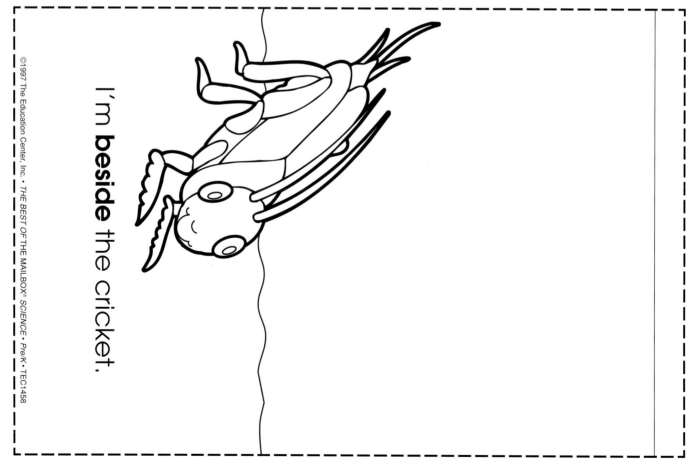

I'm **beside** the cricket.

last page

(last page)

Ladybug, where are you?

I'm home!

Use with "Insect Math" on page 98.

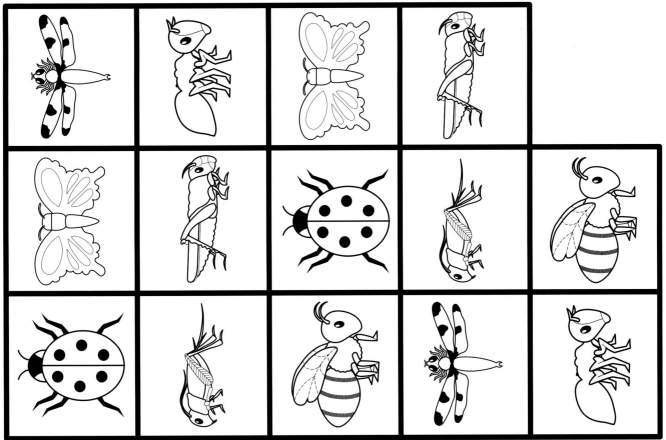

Ladybug Booklet Cover Pattern

Use with "Ladybug, Where Are You?" on page 97 and "Buggy Bulletin Board—Station One: Ladybug" on page 98.

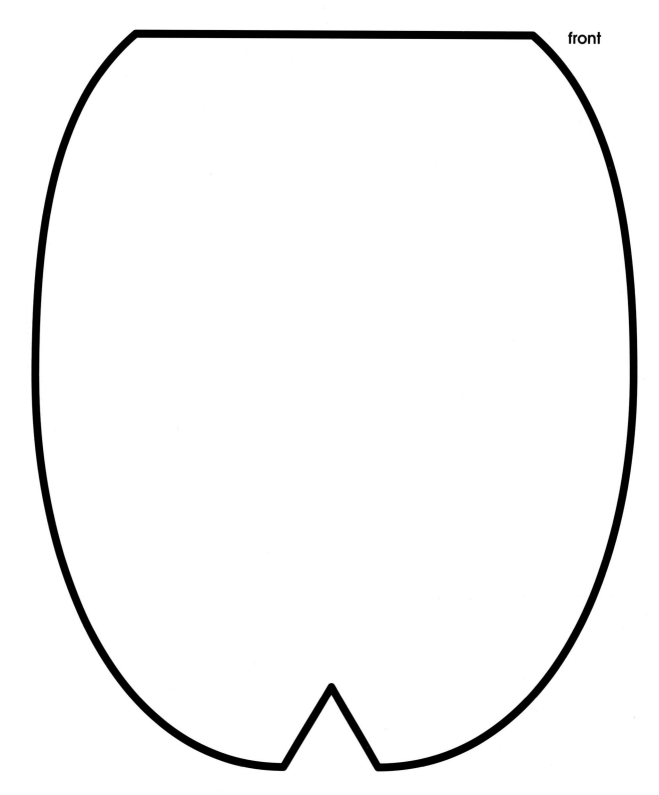

front

Ladybug Booklet Cover Pattern

Use with "Ladybug, Where Are You?" on page 97 and "Buggy Bulletin Board—Station One: Ladybug" on page 98.

back

Science For Early Childhood Teachers

Seed Secrets

Explore the secrets of seeds with this harvest of hands-on activities.

Activity 1

You will need:
brown paper lunch
 bags (one per child)
a hole puncher
twine
a marker
pencils
stencils
glue
assorted dried beans and seeds

What to do:
To make a seed sack, roll down the top of a brown paper lunch bag. Punch a hole, on each side of the bag, through the rolled portion. Thread and tie a 30-inch piece of twine through the holes. Label the seed sack as shown. Have each child trace a stencil onto his seed sack. Then have him squeeze a trail of glue along the resulting outline before covering the trail with seeds.

Have students take their seed sacks home to collect seeds for use in Activities 2 and 3.

Questions to ask:
1. Where can you find seeds?
2. Why do plants have seeds?

This is why:

Seeds are made by trees, shrubs, and soft-stemmed plants. Seeds are special parts of plants that make new plants.

Activity 2

You will need:
the seeds collected in Activity 1
paper plates (1 per group of
 youngsters)
4" poster-board squares (7–10
 per group)
glue
poster board (1 sheet per
 group)

What to do:
Divide youngsters into small groups. Have each youngster in the group select several seeds from his seed sack and place them on a paper plate in the center of the table. Allow time for each child to examine the seeds.

Questions to ask:
1. What do you notice about the seeds?
2. Why aren't all of the seeds the same?

Then:
Assist each group in selecting and gluing each of seven to ten seeds atop a different poster-board square. Have each group classify its seeds into two groups: *big* and *little*. Then have each group glue its squares onto a sheet of poster board to create a simple bar graph.

Questions to ask:
1. How did your group decide if each seed was big or little?
2. Did your group have more big seeds or more little seeds?

This is why:

Seeds are produced by thousands of different kinds of plants. Each kind of plant has its own special kind of seed.

Activity 3

You will need:
the seeds collected in Activity 1
paper plates (1 per child)
glue
4" x 12" construction-paper strips
 (one per child)

What to do:
For a seriation activity, have each child place his remaining seeds (collected in Activity 1) on a paper plate. Then have him examine his seeds to find the smallest seed. Have him glue it to the left side of a construction-paper strip. Then have him identify his largest seed and glue it to the right side of the strip. Have him select another seed to glue in between the two seeds on the strip. More advanced youngsters may glue additional seeds (arranged in sequential size order) atop their strips.

Questions to ask:
1. What kinds of plants grow from little seeds?
2. What kinds of plants grow from big seeds?

This is why:

Different kinds of plants produce seeds which vary greatly in size. The size of the seed has no relationship to the size of the plant that grows from it. Small seeds can produce large plants. The giant redwood tree, for example, grows from a seed that is only 1/16 inch long.

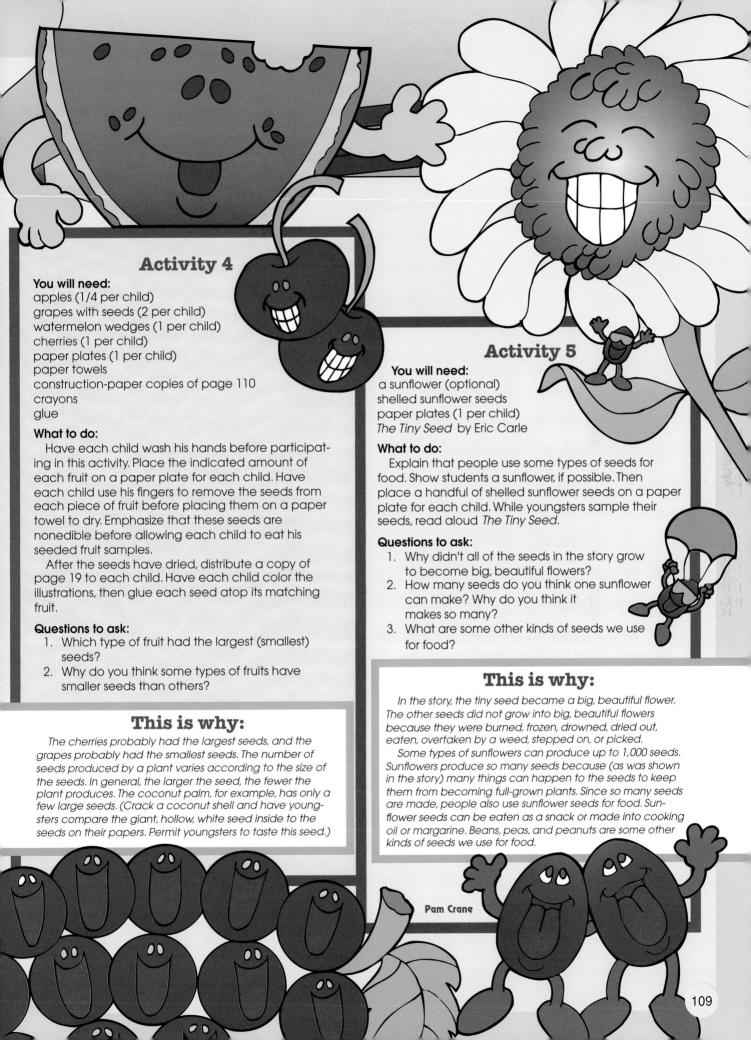

Activity 4

You will need:
apples (1/4 per child)
grapes with seeds (2 per child)
watermelon wedges (1 per child)
cherries (1 per child)
paper plates (1 per child)
paper towels
construction-paper copies of page 110
crayons
glue

What to do:
Have each child wash his hands before participating in this activity. Place the indicated amount of each fruit on a paper plate for each child. Have each child use his fingers to remove the seeds from each piece of fruit before placing them on a paper towel to dry. Emphasize that these seeds are nonedible before allowing each child to eat his seeded fruit samples.

After the seeds have dried, distribute a copy of page 19 to each child. Have each child color the illustrations, then glue each seed atop its matching fruit.

Questions to ask:
1. Which type of fruit had the largest (smallest) seeds?
2. Why do you think some types of fruits have smaller seeds than others?

This is why:

The cherries probably had the largest seeds, and the grapes probably had the smallest seeds. The number of seeds produced by a plant varies according to the size of the seeds. In general, the larger the seed, the fewer the plant produces. The coconut palm, for example, has only a few large seeds. (Crack a coconut shell and have youngsters compare the giant, hollow, white seed inside to the seeds on their papers. Permit youngsters to taste this seed.)

Activity 5

You will need:
a sunflower (optional)
shelled sunflower seeds
paper plates (1 per child)
The Tiny Seed by Eric Carle

What to do:
Explain that people use some types of seeds for food. Show students a sunflower, if possible. Then place a handful of shelled sunflower seeds on a paper plate for each child. While youngsters sample their seeds, read aloud *The Tiny Seed*.

Questions to ask:
1. Why didn't all of the seeds in the story grow to become big, beautiful flowers?
2. How many seeds do you think one sunflower can make? Why do you think it makes so many?
3. What are some other kinds of seeds we use for food?

This is why:

In the story, the tiny seed became a big, beautiful flower. The other seeds did not grow into big, beautiful flowers because they were burned, frozen, drowned, dried out, eaten, overtaken by a weed, stepped on, or picked.

Some types of sunflowers can produce up to 1,000 seeds. Sunflowers produce so many seeds because (as was shown in the story) many things can happen to the seeds to keep them from becoming full-grown plants. Since so many seeds are made, people also use sunflower seeds for food. Sunflower seeds can be eaten as a snack or made into cooking oil or margarine. Beans, peas, and peanuts are some other kinds of seeds we use for food.

Pam Crane

109

Name _____

Fruit Seeds

Color.
Glue seeds to match.

grapes

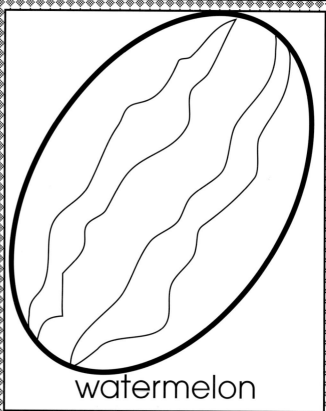

watermelon

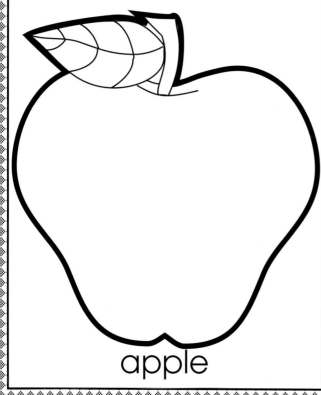

apple

cherry

Wonders Never Cease

Ready, Set, Grow!

Watch the excitement sprout as your little ones explore seeds with these hands-on activities.

Note: If you have any doubt that your seeds will germinate, try sprouting several of them between layers of moist paper towels. Test your seeds at least ten days before you plan to have students complete Activities 2 and 3.

Activity 1

You will need:
watermelon seeds (at least one per child)
apple seeds (at least one per child)
corn (at least one per child)
lima beans (at least one per child)
paper plates
magnifying glasses (optional)

What to do:
Spread the seeds out on a tabletop. Have each youngster put one seed of each kind on his paper plate. Ask students to carefully examine their seeds, preferably with a magnifying glass.

Questions to ask:
• How would you describe each seed?
• How are your seeds the same (different)?
• What fruit or vegetable did each seed probably come from?
• Why aren't all seeds the same?

This is why:
Seeds are produced by thousands of different kinds of plants. Each kind of plant has its own special kind of seed.

For added fun:
Have a seed tasting party! Have students brainstorm edible seeds as you make a list. Then have student volunteers bring edible seeds such as peanuts (to be shelled), popcorn (to be popped), or peas in pods (to be shelled and cooked).

Activity 2

You will need:
lima beans (1 per child)
lima beans that have been soaked in water overnight*
 (at least 2 per child)
*Important note: Reserve half of the soaked beans for Activity 3.

What to do:
Give each student an unsoaked lima bean.

Questions to ask:
• How would you describe this seed?
• If this seed were soaked overnight, how do you think it would change?

What to do:
Give each child a soaked bean to compare to his unsoaked one.

Questions to ask:
• How would you describe the soaked seed?
• How does it compare with the seed that wasn't soaked?
• Why does soaking a seed cause it to change?

This is why:
Seeds absorb water when they are soaked. The water causes many chemical changes inside the seed.

What to do:
Have each youngster split his soaked bean in half. Have him examine the inside of the seed.

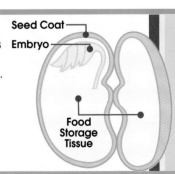

Seed Coat
Embryo
Food Storage Tissue

Questions to ask:
• What do you notice inside of the seed?
• Why do you think a seed has different parts?

This is why:
When a seed is soaked, the seed coat swells and part of the embryo begins to grow. The embryo is the part of the seed from which the mature plant develops. The food storage tissue stores food for the embryo, and the seed coat protects the embryo and food storage tissue from injury, insects, and loss of water.

Activity 3

You will need:
soaked lima beans
 (1 per child—prepared
 for Activity 2)
clear plastic cups
 (1 per child)
black construction paper
 cut to cover the cups
moist potting soil
tape
water
paper
strips of construction
 paper (5 to 6 per child)
scissors
glue

What to do:
 Have each student fill a personalized cup with soil, then insert a seed in the soil very close to the side of the cup. Wrap black construction paper around the cup and tape it in place. (Prepare a few extra seed cups since some seeds may not germinate.) Have each student lightly water or mist his cup of soil occasionally. Every other day, assist each youngster in removing (and then replacing) the paper from the side of his cup.

Question to ask:
• What happened to your bean since you last saw it?

What to do:
 Once a student's sprout is more than 1/4 inch tall, have him use a strip of paper to measure its height, cutting the strip where it touches the top of the plant. Date the strip and glue it near the left margin of a piece of paper to begin a growth chart. Every four or five days remeasure the plant and add another strip to the chart.

Questions to ask:
• What did your sprout
 look like at first?
• How did it change
 as it grew?
• Why are these changes
 taking place?
• What happens to
 change a bean
 into a plant?

Samantha's Bean Growth Chart

June 1 — June 4 — June 8 — June 11 — June 15 — June 21

This is what happens:
 The seed coat of a lima bean swells when soaked and the bean begins to sprout. The first sign of life from above will probably be the cracking of the soil. Below the surface of the soil, the roots begin to emerge from the seed. As time goes on, a white stem and leaves appear. Once the bean plant has broken the surface, it will grow measurably every four days until maturity.

Pam Crane

Activity 4

You will need:
a windy day
a gone-to-seed dandelion, a milkweed pod, or a
 mature cattail

What to do:
 On a windy day, take students outdoors. Have students blow on the dandelion (or open the milkweed pod or break the cattail into pieces).

Questions to ask:
• What happened to the seeds from the dandelion
 (or cattail or milkweed pod)?
• What other ways do seeds travel?
• Why is it important for seeds to go places?

This is why:
 The more different places seeds are dispersed, the better chance they will have of sprouting in great numbers. Wind, water, birds, fur-bearing animals, and people disperse seeds. Once they are carried to a new location, most seeds remain dormant until conditions for germination are more favorable.

Follow-Up Activities:
Read aloud and discuss Susan Kuchalla's *Now I Know All About Seeds.*

How Does Your Garden Grow?

Dig into these garden-related ideas and watch the learning opportunities in your classroom grow and grow and grow!

by Lucia Kemp Henry

Good Things From The Garden

What's so good about a garden? If you do the following activities, youngsters are sure to say, "Plenty!" Collect a wide variety of toy fruits, vegetables, and flowers. (If these items are not available, make picture cards by gluing magazine pictures onto tagboard.) Place the fruits, vegetables, and flowers in a large basket. Have youngsters look at the contents of the basket, and encourage a discussion regarding where real versions of the food items come from. Emphasize the fact that all of these foods grow from seeds that have been planted in some type of garden. Then ask students to sort the foods according to whatever categories they can think of. Encourage lots of creative ways of categorizing. Next ask students to finish up by placing all of the flowers in a vase, the fruits in a bowl, and the vegetables in a basket. Isn't it easy to see what's so good about a garden?

Follow up this activity by reading aloud Lois Ehlert's *Eating The Alphabet* (Harcourt Brace Jovanovich). As you read, ask children to determine in which category—fruit or vegetable—each featured item belongs. A beautiful sampling of flower illustrations can also be explored in Lois Ehlert's *Planting A Rainbow* (Harcourt Brace Jovanovich).

Garden Song

Creating a garden is a lot of hard work—and there are so many jobs to do! Tomie dePaola's *Too Many Hopkins* (Putnam) illustrates this point just perfectly. After sharing *Too Many Hopkins*, engage your students in a discussion about all the tasks that need to be done to create and maintain a garden. Ask youngsters if they can think of any additional tasks to add to the list. Then teach your children the song below and have them pantomime the actions as everyone sings together.

(Sung to the tune of "Here We Go Round The Mulberry Bush")
This is the way we **dig the soil,**
Dig the soil, dig the soil.
This is the way we **dig the soil—**
A-workin' in the garden.

Repeat the song, replacing the boldfaced phrases with each of these tasks in turn: rake the soil, make the rows, plant the seeds, water the seeds, pull the weeds, gather the food.

Hands-On Gardening—Anytime!

Inspire the gardening mood in your little ones by reading aloud *A Very Young Gardener* by Jill Krementz (Dial Books For Young Readers). After discussing the book, convert your sand table into a classroom gardening plot. Provide garden tools and props such as garden gloves, small garden trowels, watering cans, and a basket or crate of "seedlings" clipped from sections of artificial greenery. Also include craft sticks, magazine pictures, crayons, construction paper, scissors, and tape for students to use to make garden markers.

Have students work in the garden in pairs. Ask youngsters to plan and plant a garden using the materials provided. As the seedlings are being planted, encourage children to make garden markers by coloring or cutting out pictures of what the pretend plants will grow up to be. Then have the children tape each picture to a different craft stick. Take a photograph of each gardening team and their garden. Display the photographs on a bulletin board along with each team's description of their garden and their gardening experience.

113

Seed Sorts

Seeds come in an astounding array of sorts and sizes, and this activity will help bring that concept into focus. Collect a variety of seeds that are large enough for youngsters to handle. You could visit a seed store and/or save seeds from peaches, apricots, apples, grapefruit, watermelons, sunflowers, and pumpkins. Place all of the seeds in a center along with pieces of tagboard and glue. As a child visits the center, have him sort the seeds. Ask him to take one of each type of seed and arrange the seeds according to size. Then have him glue the seeds on the tagboard. If desired, have each child write (or dictate) a sentence on the tagboard.

Seeds have a skazillion sizes!

Luke

Watch It Grow

If you do this bean-planting activity with your youngsters, it will seem as though you can just about *see* the plants growing right before your very eyes! For each child, you will need a lima bean seed that has been soaked in water overnight, a clear plastic cup, and potting soil. Also provide a water-filled plant sprayer. Have each child fill a personalized cup with soil, then plant a soaked seed very close to the side of the cup. (Prepare a few extra seed cups since some seeds may not germinate.) Direct each child to lightly water or mist his cup of soil occasionally so that the soil stays moist, but not soaked. Each day, have youngsters observe their cups to see what's happening! Extend this activity by reading aloud *How A Seed Grows* by Helene J. Jordan (Thomas Y. Crowell Company) and *The Carrot Seed* by Ruth Krauss (Harper & Row). Have youngsters compare and contrast the events in each of the books with what is happening in their own bean cups.

Katie

My Seed

After planting seeds and watching them grow (see "Watch It Grow"), each child will have the information he needs to author his own booklet about how seeds grow. For each child, duplicate the patterns (pages 117–121) on white construction paper. Read, discuss, and complete one page at a time (see the directions below). Then cut out each page along the bold outline. Fold the top of the page down along the shaded fold line. Cut out the accompanying text box (on page 117) and glue it to the folded top section. When all of the pages have been completed, color and cut out the cover (page 117). If desired, glue seeds onto the cover. Stack the pages in order and staple them together along the left edge. Keep these booklets available for free-time reading and encourage youngsters to share their booklets with one another.

Page One: Read the text box (page 117) for page 1. Draw a seed in the ground. Discuss what the seed might grow into and draw a small picture of this on the garden marker. Complete the sentence at the top of the page. Color the page.

Page Two: Read the text box (page 117) for page 2. Draw roots growing from the seed. Write a sentence to tell what happened to the seed. Color the garden marker and the page.

Page Three: Read the text box (page 117) for page 3. Draw and color the sun and a shoot pushing through the ground. Write a sentence to tell what happened in the picture. Color the garden marker and the page.

Page Four: Read the text box (page 117) for page 4. Draw a big plant or flower. Color the garden marker and the page.

My Seed

By Meredith Andrews

Draw a seed in the ground.
Draw a picture on the marker.
Write.
My seed will become a
tomato

Plant a seed
in nice, warm soil
and pat it down just so.

1

Plant Pot Craft

These designer plant pots make great decorations or supply holders to spruce up your classroom during your garden theme. In advance, collect a small clay flowerpot for each child. Spray-paint each pot with white spray paint. When the paint is dry, give each child a pot and have him visit one or more of the stations described below to decorate his pot. The finished products just might be so impressive that you'll want to make more for Father's Day or other special occasions!

Station One: Provide a colorful supply of assorted dried beans and craft glue. Have children glue the beans onto the pots.

Station Two: Provide various shapes of sponge cutouts and acrylic paints. Have children decorate their pots with sponge prints.

Station Three: Provide a supply of decorative napkins and/or tissue paper and paintbrushes. Have children use polyurethane to paint on torn pieces of the napkins or tissue paper.

Our Secret Gardens

Because of the popular movie and book, *The Secret Garden,* few children need to be coaxed into imagining what a secret garden might be like. So create this beautiful display to lend that "secret-garden" kind of feeling to your classroom. Duplicate the watering-can pattern (page 122) on colorful construction paper for each child. Give each student a large sheet of art paper and colorful art supplies such as construction paper, tissue paper, fabric pieces, and paints. Ask each child to use these supplies to create a picture of his secret garden. When the gardens are complete, have each child cut out his watering can and write (or dictate) about his garden. Display each child's secret garden near his watering can on a bulletin board. Oooh—the secret's out!

My secret garden has a mountain in the middle of it.

Noah

115

Grandma's Garden

This fun and challenging game will help expand young-sters' thinking about what can be found in a garden, as well as stretch those memory skills! Seat children in a circle. Begin by saying, "I went to Grandma's garden and brought back [insert a garden item such as a carrot]." Have the child to your right say, "I went to Grandma's garden and brought back [insert the teacher's item] and some [add another garden item such as daisies]." Continue around the circle in the same manner, having each child repeat the items that were named before his turn, and then add one.

You can add to the challenge of this game by playing Grandma's Alphabet Garden. In this version of the game, each player must add a new item in alphabetical order (for example, "I went to Grandma's alphabet garden and brought back an apple, a butterfly, a carrot, some dirt, an eggplant,…").

The Garden Gourmet

To culminate your garden theme, plan to have a garden feast. On a specified day, ask each child to bring in a food item that comes from a garden—in one way or another! Explain that any food item is acceptable—as long as its owner can explain how the item relates to a garden. To inspire youngsters, suggest items that might not typically be thought of as coming from a garden. (For example, potato chips would be an acceptable garden item because they are made from potatoes that are grown in a garden!) After each garden item is approved, have each child use a craft stick and construction paper to make a garden marker for his item. Then cover a long table with a tablecloth. Have the children arrange their items and garden markers in rows. Then, of course—dig in!

More Literature Links

Anna's Garden Songs
Written by Mary Q. Steele
Illustrated by Lena Anderson
Published by Greenwillow Books

The Victory Garden Vegetable Alphabet Book
Written by Jerry Pallota and Bob Thomson
Illustrated by Edgar Stewart
Published by Charlesbridge

Growing Vegetable Soup
Written & Illustrated by Lois Ehlert
Published by Harcourt Brace Jovanovich

Vegetable Garden
Written & Illustrated by Douglas Florian
Published by Harcourt Brace Jovanovich

Booklet Cover And Text Boxes

1

Plant a seed
in nice, warm soil
and pat it down just so.

2

The roots will sprout
below the ground.
That's how plants start to
grow.

3

Sun and water
help it grow
a little bit each day...

4

until the plant
is big and tall
and strong in every way.

My Seed

By _____

Draw a seed in the ground.
Draw a picture on the marker.
Write.
My seed will become a

Staple here.

1

Draw roots growing from the seed.
Write. Tell what happened to the seed.

Staple here.

2

Draw the sun.
Draw a shoot.
Write. Tell what happened.

Staple here.

3

Booklet Page

Draw a big plant.

Staple here.

4

Pattern
Watering can
Use with "Our Secret Gardens" on page 115.

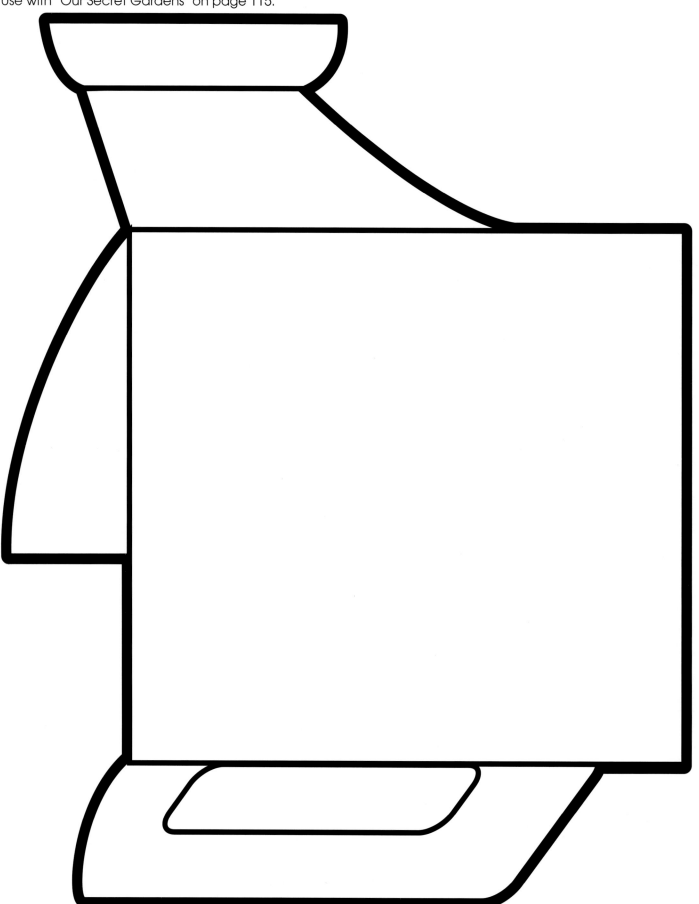

©1997 The Education Center, Inc. • *THE BEST OF* THE MAILBOX® *SCIENCE* • *Pre/K* • TEC1458

Splash!

You won't have to fish for compliments when you fill your youngsters' days with these fun fish activities. Keep them hooked with lots of arts-and-crafts projects, literature-related activities, writing opportunities, poems, a song, and a fishy foldout book.

by Lucia Kemp Henry

A School Of Swimmers

A whole school of puppet fish are irresistible bait for getting youngsters hooked on the topic of fish. To make quick work of this puppet-making project, recruit a few parent volunteers to cut out the felt pieces and assist with assembly. Have the adults use one color of felt and the body pattern on page 127 to make two fish body cutouts per child. From a contrasting color of felt, have volunteers cut out two tail pieces, one top fin, and one bottom fin for each child's puppet. When it's time to assemble the puppets, have an adult assist each youngster as he uses craft glue to glue a top and bottom fin within the perimeter of one of the fish body pieces. Then have each student run a trail of glue around the inside perimeter of his fish-body cutout, leaving the straight edge without glue. Instruct him to place the second fish body cutout on the first one. Complete the construction of the fish by having youngsters position each of the tail cutouts over the body section as shown. Glue the tails only to the body—not to each other. Set the fish aside to dry. On another day, have students use craft glue to attach button eyes and sequined tail and fin accents. Also provide fabric paints in squeeze bottles for adding finishing touches.

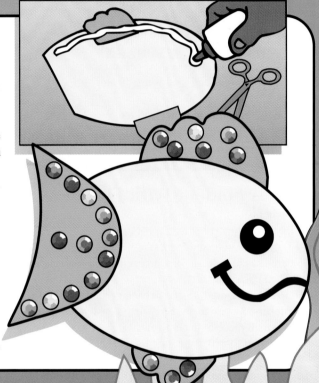

A Fishy Tune

Once your children are equipped with splendid fish puppets (see "A School Of Swimmers"), they'll be eager to put them to use. Make a big splash by introducing this lively song to the tune of "Did You Ever See A Lassie?" Soon each of your little ones can manipulate their puppets and imagine what it's like to swim, swish, slide, and splash through ocean currents.

Did You Ever See A Fishy?
(sung to the tune of "Did You Ever See A Lassie?")

Did you ever see a fishy,
A fishy, a fishy?
Did you ever see a fishy
Swim this way and that?
Swim this way and that way
And that way and this way?
Did you ever see a fishy
Swim this way and that?

(Repeat the song replacing the boldfaced word with each of these words in turn: *swish, slide,* and *splash*.)

Barry Slate

123

Five Funny Fish

Divide your youngsters into groups of five to act out this counting poem. Students are certain to get a lot of fun from saying the poem if each of them has a fish puppet for acting it out. Refer to "A School Of Swimmers" on page 123 for puppet assembly directions. As students stand in groups of five and say the poem with you, direct them to use their fish puppets or hands to illustrate the words. After asking one child in each group to sit, repeat the poem, replacing the word *five* with *four* and modifying the movements accordingly. Ask another child in each group to sit, and repeat the poem as before, substituting *three* for *four* and modifying the movements accordingly. Continue play in this manner, changing the numeral words and movements, until no students remain standing.

Five Funny Fish

Splish, splash, splish!	*Move fish puppet rapidly from side-to-side.*
See the funny fish.	*Point to fish puppet.*
Five funny fish in the sea.	*Hold up five fingers.*
Swim up and down.	*Make up and down movements with puppet.*
Swim all around.	*"Swim" puppet all around.*
Five funny fish in the sea.	*Hold up five fingers.*

by Lucia Kemp Henry

A Foldout With Fins

This whopper of a fish book will no doubt be the catch of the day. On white construction paper, reproduce pages 128–131 for each student. To make a booklet, begin by cutting around the bold outlines on each of the reproduced pages. Then color the two fish-shaped cutouts (from pages 128 and 131) as desired. Decorate each of the fish's scales with a rubber-stamped or sponge-printed design. Or glue a sequin or small piece of paper to each scale. Glue all four cutouts together to make one long fish. When each child has constructed his fish, have him read and illustrate each of the programmed boxes. Help each youngster accordion-fold his book. These big foldout fish books are too big to go unnoticed for long. Before you know it your little ones will have lots of opportunities to "read" them and explain how they were made.

The One That Got Away

Use the fish patterns (pages 128 and 131), along with a long strip of bulletin-board paper, to create a really lengthy format for your youngsters' written expression. With your little ones, brainstorm words that they might use to describe a big, long, colorful fish. Write each suggestion on a fish-shaped word card, using the flash card pattern located on page 133. Cut out copies of the fish front and tail patterns (pages 128 and 131) and glue them to a strip of six-inch-wide bulletin-board paper. Begin the fish tale by writing "The fish was..." on the left end of the strip. Include the adjectives your youngsters suggested as you write one long descriptive sentence. For each word, use a color, size, and style of printing to reinforce its meaning. Post this fabulous fish tidbit, and others similar to it, on a wall. Can't you almost hear some child say, "If you think that's something, you should see the one that got away"?

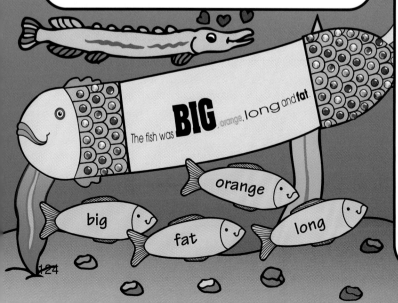

124

A Fishbowl World

Adapt a traditional waxed-paper art technique to create see-through fishbowls full of underwater color. To begin, cut out two construction-paper copies of the fishbowl pattern located on page 132. Stack the cutouts and fold them in half before cutting along the dotted lines so that two fishbowl-shaped frames remain when the paper is unfolded. Draw and cut out a fish shape, or use the sponge-printer pattern (on page 133) to create a fish cutout. Fold an 11 1/2" x 15" sheet of waxed paper in half. Unfold the waxed paper. Scatter crayon shavings in a small area near the fold. Arrange some cellophane grass or tissue-paper strips so that they extend upward from the fold. Place the fish cutout about 1/2" above the crayon shavings before refolding the paper. Momentarily center one of the fishbowl cutouts over the waxed-paper scene to verify that the art is positioned correctly. Remove the fishbowl and place the waxed-paper scene between newspaper sheets. Quickly iron the entire waxed-paper surface with a warm iron (low setting). Spread glue on one side of each fishbowl cutout. Sandwich the waxed-paper art between the cutouts, and trim away the excess waxed paper. Tape students' completed fishbowls to a window or suspend them from the ceiling on strings.

Flashy Fish

These fantasy fish look "mah-velous" on a bright blue bulletin-board sea. To make a fish, draw or trace a large basic fish shape onto tagboard. Select two shades of the same color of tissue paper; then cut the paper into small squares. Using a large paintbrush and white glue thinned with water, coat the fish with glue. Place one tissue-paper square at a time within the fish-shaped outline, allowing the squares to overlap. Continue to add squares and glue (if necessary) until the entire cutout is covered. Coat the project with a final layer of glue. Allow the glue to dry completely before cutting along the outline. To create the fish's tail, staple several one-inch-wide strips of tissue paper to the tail area of the cutout. Staple shorter strips to the cutout to create fins. For the fish's eye, glue on a gold foil circle or a sequin. When mounting the fish on a bulletin board, staple the strips of paper that form the tail and fins so that they are not flush with the board's surface. The flashy three-dimensional effect of these fish is sure to lure more than a few fishing enthusiasts to take a closer look.

Fish Food

The catch-of-the-day is this fish-shaped sandwich. Have your young chefs cut fish shapes from slices of wheat bread. Then obtain their assistance in making a bowl of tuna salad. Ask each child to spread a slice of fish-shaped bread with tuna salad. To complete the fish sandwich, have him add a slice of a pimento-filled green olive for the fish's eye. This treat will go well with a few small, fish-shaped pretzels.

Souvenirs Of A Splashy Unit

This fish unit souvenir will fit your students to a *T*. Ask each youngster to bring to school an undecorated, prewashed T-shirt. (Have a few spare shirts on hand for those who are unable to bring their own shirts.) Using the sponge-printer pattern (on page 133) as a guide, cut a sponge into a fish shape. Slide a piece of cardboard inside a shirt to prevent bleed through and to provide a firm surface for printing. In a shallow container, mix fabric or acrylic paint with textile medium. Have each child in turn press the fish-shaped sponge into the paint, onto a scrap-paper blotter, then onto his shirt to create several fish designs. Encourage students to embellish their fish designs as desired using additional fabric paints. Allow the shirts to dry before following the paint manufacturer's directions for permanently setting the paint.

Sizing Up The School

Use the school of variously sized fish featured on pages 157 and 159 for lots of flannelboard fun. Prepare the fish for flannelboard use by cutting them out and backing them with felt or sandpaper. Then have student volunteers place the fish one-by-one on a flannelboard, working from smallest to largest as you recite the following rhyme together:

That's About The Size Of It

Once there was a teeny fish
A-swimmin' in the sea.
Said the teeny fish,
"Oh, how I wish,
To see a fish bigger than me!"

Repeat the poem four more times, replacing the word teeny *with each of these words in turn:* little, average, big, *and* huge. *Then read the final verse which follows.*

Once there was a giant fish
A-swimmin' in the sea.
Said the giant fish,
"There are no fish
As big or as gorgeous as me!"
by Lucia Kemp Henry

Literature List

Swimmy
Written & Illustrated by Leo Lionni
Published by Pantheon

The Rainbow Fish
Written & Illustrated by Marcus Pfister
Translated by J. Alison James
Published by North-South Books

Fish Eyes: A Book You Can Count On
Written & Illustrated by Lois Ehlert
Published by Harcourt Brace Jovanovich, Publishers

Big Al
Written by Andrew Clements
Illustrated by Yoshi
Published by Picture Book Studio

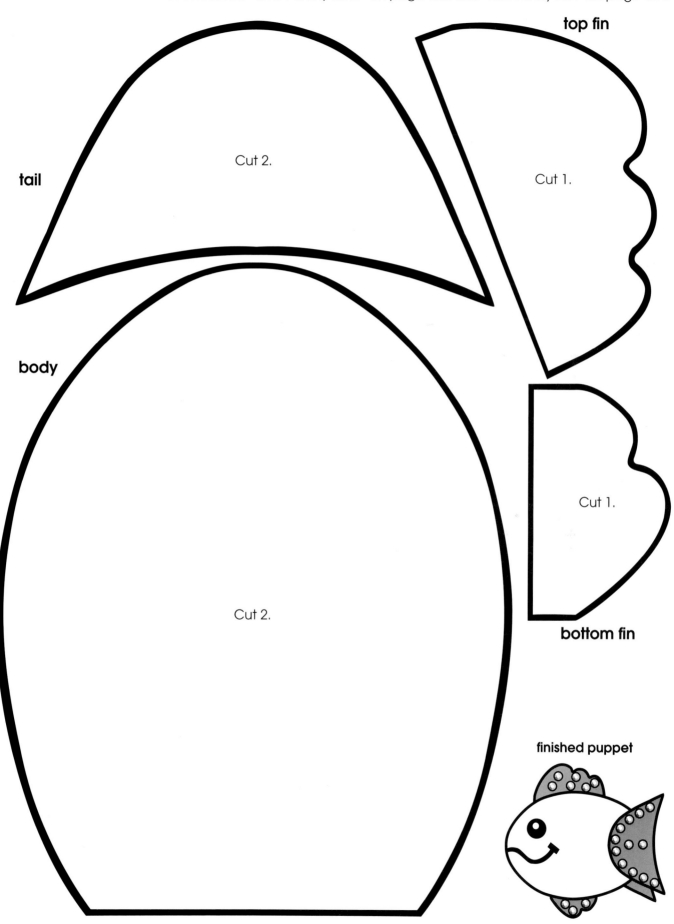

top fin

Cut 1.

tail

Cut 2.

body

Cut 1.

Cut 2.

bottom fin

finished puppet

Fish Front Pattern

Use with "A Foldout With Fins" and "The One That Got Away" on page 124.

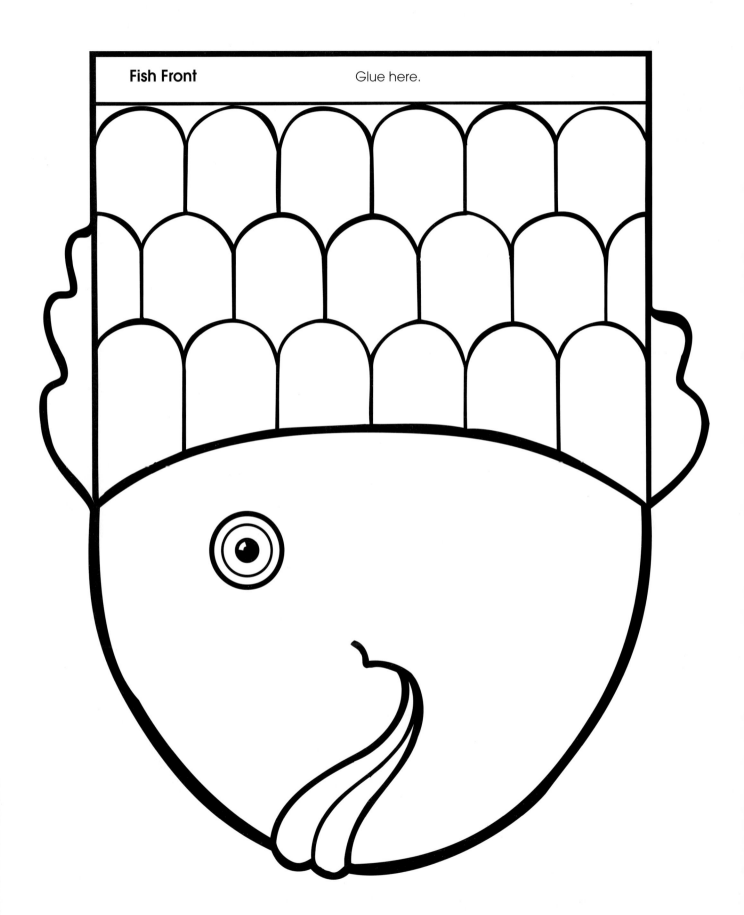

Fish Front

Glue here.

Page 1   Glue here.

Yellow fish.

Blue fish.

One fish.

Two fish.

Pattern

Use with "A Foldout With Fins" on page 124.

Page 2

Glue here.

Big fish.

Teeny fish.

Funny fish.

Meanie fish.

©The Education Center, Inc.

Fishbowl Pattern

Use with "A Fishbowl World" on page 125.

Finished Project

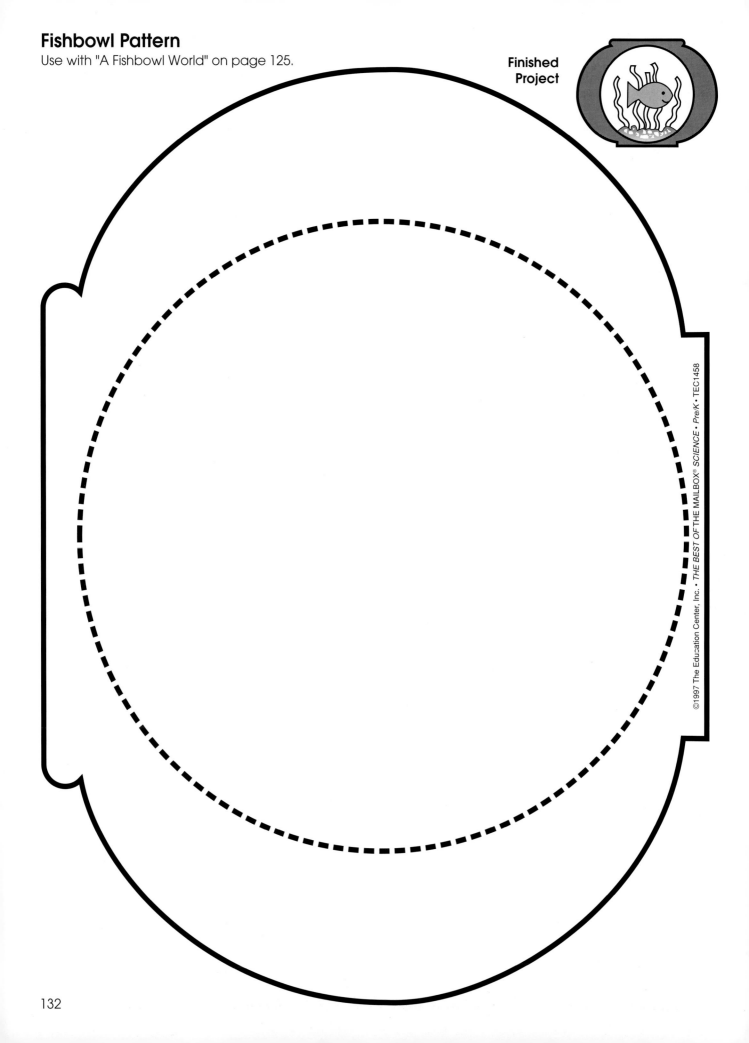

Patterns

Fishbowl Nametag

Duplicate and program with students' names or program for use with games or centers.

Fish Sponge Printer

Use with "A Fishbowl World" on page 125 and "Souvenirs Of A Splashy Unit" on page 126.

Fish Flash Card

Use with "The One That Got Away" on page 124.

Goldfish Award

Duplicate and present to students for exceptional behavior.

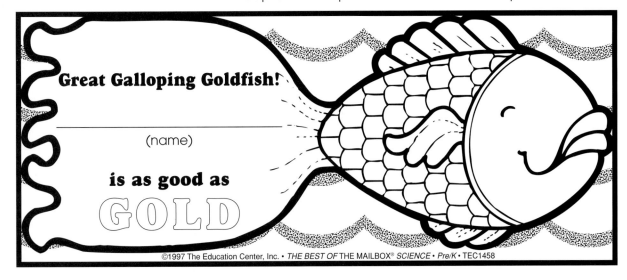

Great Galloping Goldfish!

_____
(name)

is as good as

GOLD

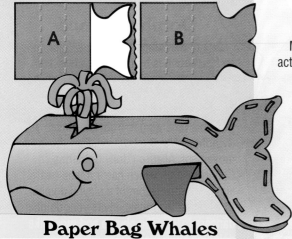

Paper Bag Whales

Your little ones can make some cute cetaceans using paper bags and construction paper scraps. To make a whale, place an unopened, brown lunch bag on a table. Near the top of the bag, place and trace the fluke pattern (page 144). Remove the pattern and cut along the traced lines through all thicknesses. For the blowhole, cut a small *X* in the bag. Open the bag, and stuff it lightly (about 3/4 of the way full) with tissue or newspaper. Staple the fluke ends closed; then staple along the sides of the fluke. Staple the remaining openings as shown. Use markers to draw a mouth and eyes. Roll up a 4 1/2" x 12" piece of blue construction paper to form a cylinder that is 4 1/2 inches tall. Glue or tape the paper so it can't unroll. Snip one end of the cylinder several times, cutting only about halfway down. Curl the fringed ends to resemble a waterspout before inserting the spout into the blowhole. Cut two flippers (patterns on page 144) from paper scraps and glue them to the whale's sides.

Whales In A Bottle

Whether your youngsters assist you in making one of these whale tanks or they each make individual ones to keep, this project is going to make a big splash. Remove the black plastic bottom from a two-liter soft-drink bottle for this activity. Fill the bottle about one-quarter full of water. Tint the water with food coloring and add a drop of liquid detergent. Drop in a few pieces of aquarium gravel. For whales, inflate two small blue balloons, release most of the air, and tie the ends closed. Push the balloons into the bottle and screw the cap on tightly. Children will enjoy tilting these bottles back and forth to watch their whales swim.

Ruthann Hardy Szanati
Alpha, NJ

Splashin' Around

Most kinds of whales travel together in groups called *pods*. Dive into these movement activities with your classroom pod of whale imitators.

- Group students into pairs and have each pair lie on the floor with "flukes" (feet) touching. Have each pair of fluke-connected students attempt to roll across the floor without breaking the fluke connection.
- Group students into pairs and give each pair a ball. Ask each pair to work cooperatively to hold a ball between their backs. Once this is accomplished, have them try holding the ball between their foreheads, chests, and stomachs.
- Designate four students to be a whale pod. Have three of the whales leave the room while the fourth hides. When the pod returns to find their missing member, they must stay together holding hands while looking for the missing whale. The pod forms a circle around the hiding member when he is found. Play continues in this manner with new groups of students taking turns. Add another element of fun by playing Raffi's "Baby Beluga" as each pod searches.
- Form one large whale pod in this whale pod roundup. Set the mood by playing music, if desired. To begin have each youngster "swim" slowly around the room. Call out, "Whales, find a friend." At this signal, each youngster pairs up with another. When this is done, pairs of youngsters swim around the room together. Then call out, "Whales, find some friends!" Each whale pair joins with another pair and resumes swimming. Continue until one large pod is formed.

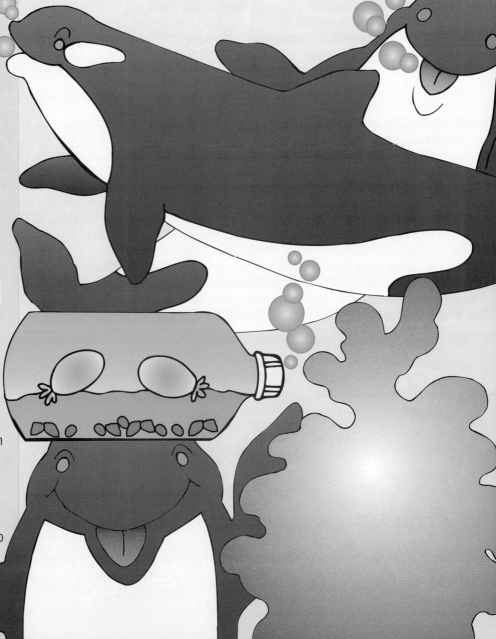

Patterns

Use with "Whale Counting Rhyme" on page 135.
Enlarge to use with "Artistic Display" on page 135.

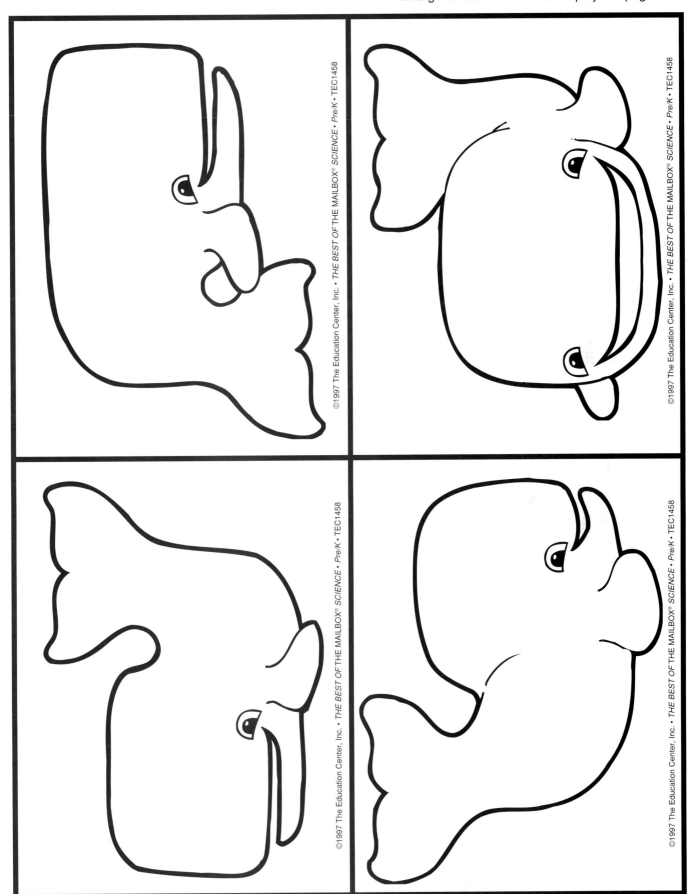

©1997 The Education Center, Inc. • *THE BEST OF THE MAILBOX® SCIENCE* • *Pre/K* • TEC1458

©1997 The Education Center, Inc. • *THE BEST OF THE MAILBOX® SCIENCE* • *Pre/K* • TEC1458

©1997 The Education Center, Inc. • *THE BEST OF THE MAILBOX® SCIENCE* • *Pre/K* • TEC1458

©1997 The Education Center, Inc. • *THE BEST OF THE MAILBOX® SCIENCE* • *Pre/K* • TEC1458

137

Whale Watcher's Guide

138

Note To The Teacher: Use with "Whale Watcher's Guide" on page 135. Enlarge to use with "Artistic Display" on page 135.

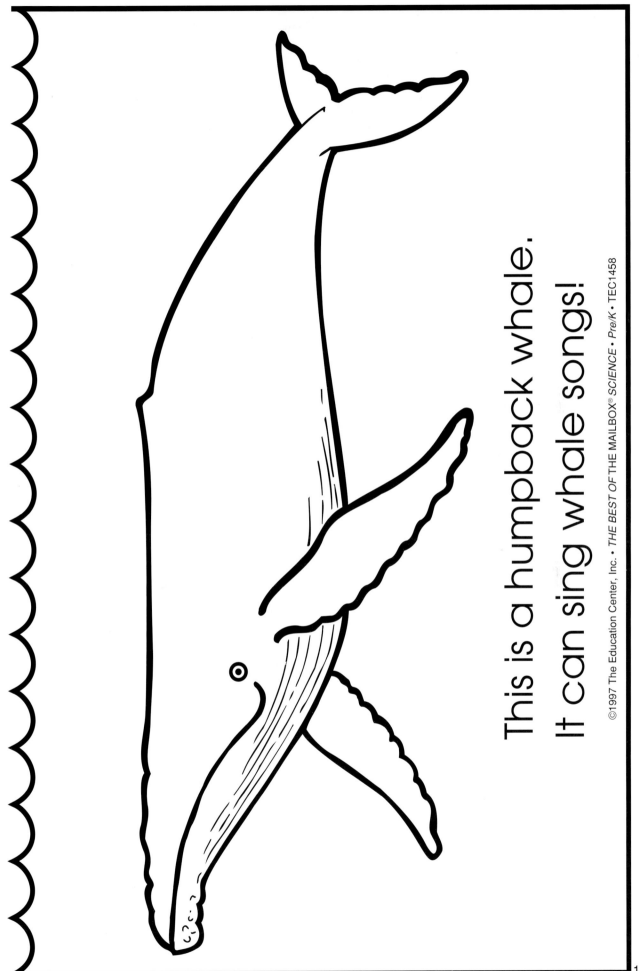

This is a humpback whale.
It can sing whale songs!

Note To The Teacher: Use with "The Expedition" on page 134 and "Whale Watcher's Guide" on page 135.

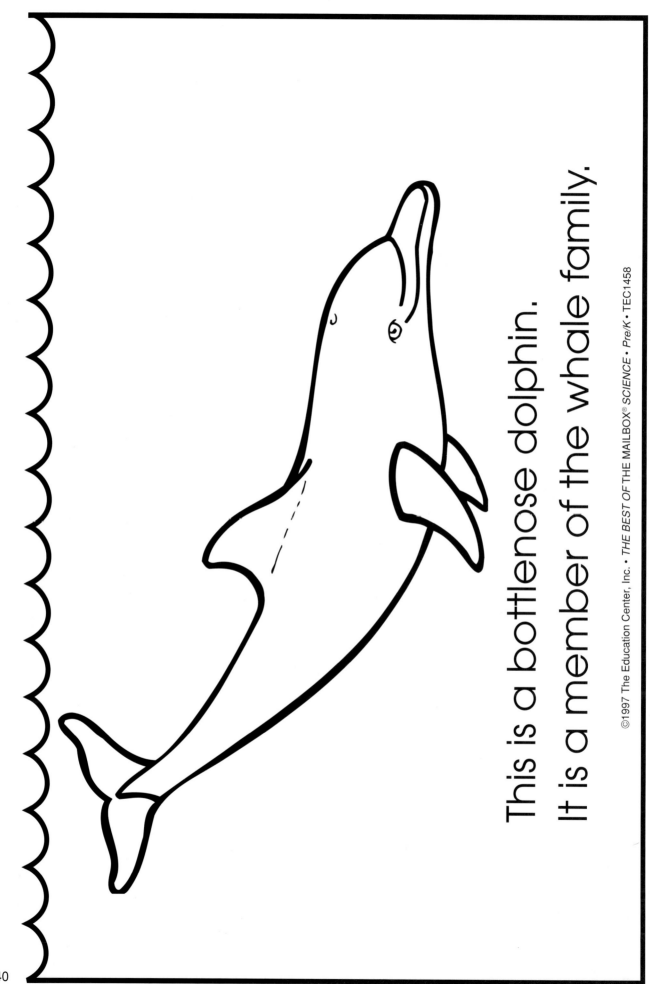

This is a bottlenose dolphin.
It is a member of the whale family.

Note To The Teacher: Use with "The Expedition" on page 134 and "Whale Watcher's Guide" on page 135.

This is an orca whale.
It is black and white.

©1997 The Education Center, Inc. • *THE BEST OF THE MAILBOX® SCIENCE* • *Pre/K* • TEC1458

Note To The Teacher: Use with "The Expedition" on page 134 and "Whale Watcher's Guide" on page 135.

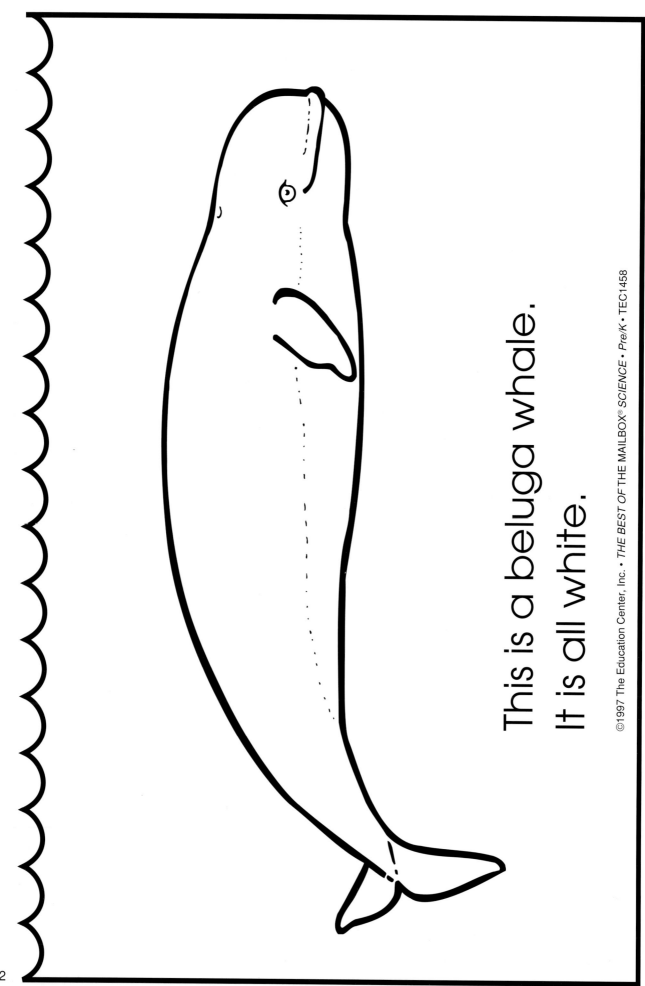

This is a beluga whale.
It is all white.

Note To The Teacher: Use with "The Expedition" on page 134 and "Whale Watcher's Guide" on page 135.

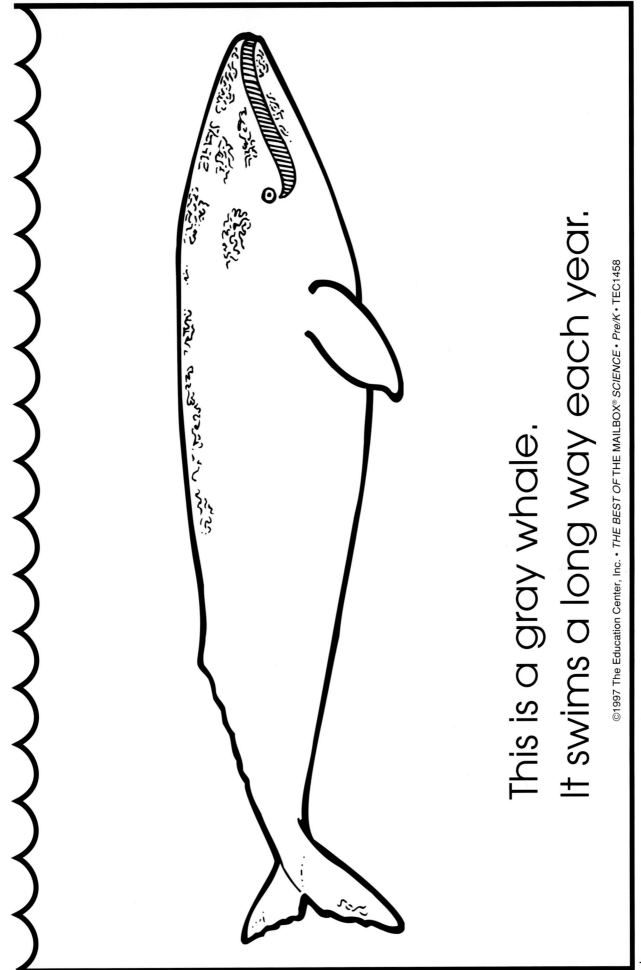

This is a gray whale.
It swims a long way each year.

Note To The Teacher: Use with "The Expedition" on page 134 and "Whale Watcher's Guide" on page 135.

Pattern

Use with "Paper Bag Whales" on page 136.

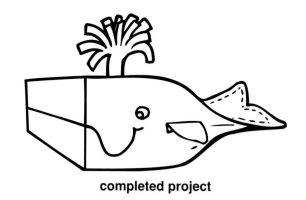

completed project

flippers

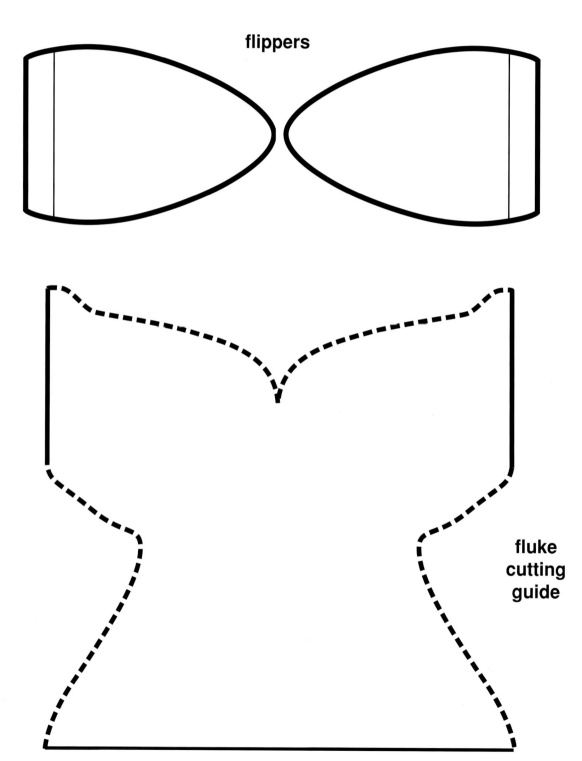

**fluke
cutting
guide**

Owl Cutouts

Use with "Flannelboard Fun" on page 27, or use these owls to decorate a small bulletin board.

Burrowing Owl

Great Horned Owl

Pygmy Owl

Use with "Flannelboard Fun" on page 27, or use these owls to decorate a small bulletin board.

Snowy Owl

Barn Owl

I live near a river. My mom knew it was time to dig my *egg* out of the mud. She knew because I was "barking." When I was out of the *egg*, she carried me to the river for my first swim.

Nile crocodile

I live in Africa. I hatched from the biggest kind of *egg*. It weighed about three pounds. When I came out of the *egg*, I was about a foot tall.

ostrich

I live in India. The *egg* I hatched from had a tough, leathery shell. My mom laid nearly 100 others. She stayed coiled around us until we hatched. When I hatched, I was 2 1/2 feet long.

Indian rock python

I live in a garden. My mom covered at least 100 eggs with a silk covering called an *egg sac*. When it got warm, all the babies tore out of the sac. I have eight legs and eight eyes.

garden spider

Use with "Guessing Game" on page 74. These cards have been designed as discussion starters. The animals are neither drawn to scale nor shown in realistic colors. Some of the eggs mentioned on these cards bear no resemblance to the design on the egg pocket.

Note:

I live on a farm. When I was ready to hatch, I began to say, "Cheep, cheep." Then I cracked my egg with my beak. I am yellow and fluffy.

chicken

I live in the ocean. My mom weaves and glues tiny eggs together to make strings of eggs. Then she hangs them from the ceiling of an ocean cave. She blows water on them and waves through them with her tentacles. This keeps the eggs clean.

octopus

I live in the ocean. My mom puts more than 200 eggs in my dad's pouch. His pouch is like a kangaroo's pouch. As the eggs in his pouch grow, his belly gets bigger and bigger.

sea horse

I live near a pond. I hatched from an egg that had a gooey covering. My egg and a thousand others floated together in the pond. The eggs were covered in jelly. The jelly helped keep us warm.

frog

Note: These cards have been designed as discussion starters. The animals are neither drawn to scale nor shown in realistic colors. Some of the eggs mentioned on these cards bear no resemblance to the design on the egg pocket.

Use with "Guessing Game" on page 74.

Cut out these insects for flannelboard or bulletin-board use. Use with "I'd Like To Introduce You!" on page 96.

butterfly

ant

bumblebee

Cut out these insects for flannelboard or bulletin-board use. Use with "I'd Like To Introduce You!" on page 96.

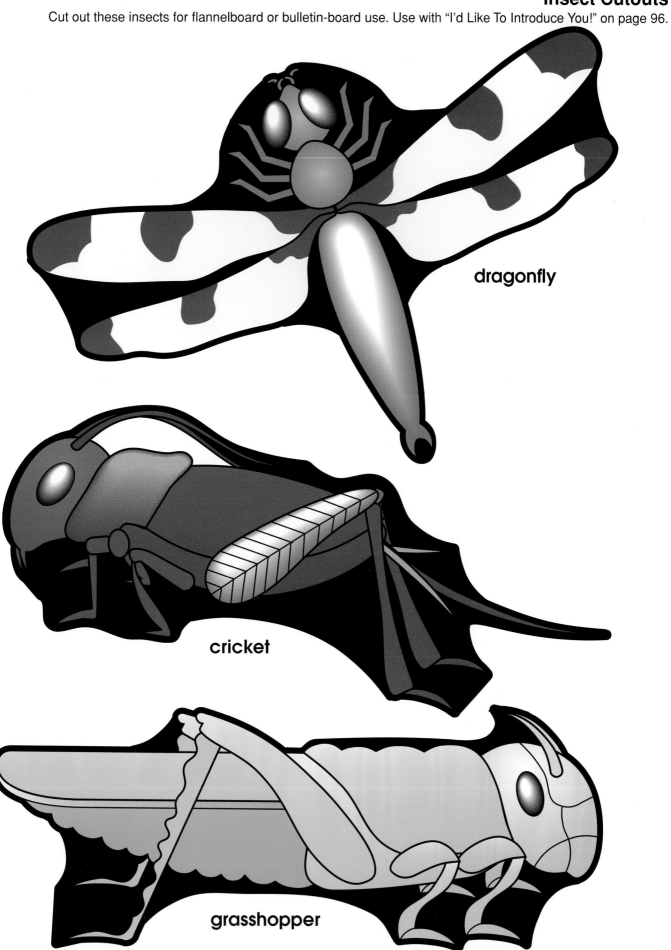

dragonfly

cricket

grasshopper

Fish Cutouts
Use with "Sizing Up The School"
on page 126.

big

average

teeny

little

giant

huge